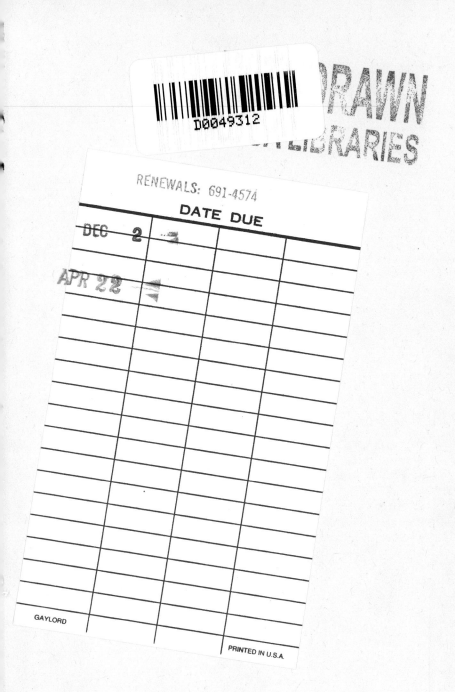

ARMIES
AND SOCIETIES
IN EUROPE,
1494–1789

ANDRÉ CORVISIER

ARMIES AND SOCIETIES IN EUROPE, 1494-1789

Translated by Abigail T. Siddall

INDIANA UNIVERSITY PRESS
BLOOMINGTON AND LONDON

Copyright © 1979 by Indiana University Press
Originally published under the title of
Armées et sociétés en Europe de 1494 à 1789:
Copyright © 1976.
Published by arrangement with
Presses Universitaires de France, Paris.

Library of Congress Cataloging in Publication Data

Corvisier, André.
Armies and societies in Europe, 1494–1789.
Translation of Armées et sociétés en Europe de 1494 à 1789.
Bibliography: p.
Includes index.
1. Armies—History.   2. Europe—History, Military.
3. Sociology, Military.   I.   Title.
UA646.C6813   301.5'93'094   78-62419
ISBN 0-253-12985-0   1 2 3 4 5 83 82 81 80 79

Contents

PREFACE

The history of military men is closely linked to military history, and because of this psychological factors (mental and moral attributes, training, attitudes) have been studied from the point of view of an army's goals and often in the hope of making predictions. Regarded as a part of military history, the study of military personnel has shared the popular and scholarly favor or disfavor accorded to the larger discipline.

It became evident very early that scholars could not study military history without considering relationships between armies and societies. Particular attention has been paid to the circumstances following defeats, for example in Prussia after Jena and in France after 1870 or 1940. And until recently historians were primarily interested in officers. The introduction of compulsory military service occasioned modest efforts toward a study of the men, reaching no farther into the past, however, than the French Revolution and the Napoleonic wars. For the ancien regime and its soldiers, labeled somewhat overhastily as "mercenaries," historians have been satisfied with reproducing traditional images.

Curiously enough, in the decade before the Second World War, totalitarian regimes, in an effort to exalt the military past of their nations or the virtues of their races, favored military history and opened it up to broader study of the troops. Unfortunately the value of this abundant historical production is seriously compromised by the ideologies of the regimes—Nazi or fascist—which pervade it.

At the end of the war, while the German school of history collapsed, military history was reawakening elsewhere, particularly in England. This time the ancien regime was to receive greater attention. Linking the history of institutions to social history, English historians published excellent studies of the military organization unique to Great Britain from the sixteenth century on, later moving beyond the limitations of their own national history. A few years later French historians followed suit, sometimes emphasizing relationships between the army and society and sometimes analyzing the composition of the army, making use of the many volumes of somewhat forbidding troop registers. Impressed by the collapse of 1945, German historians after a few years of inactivity began to consider the relationships between the army and society more closely.

At present, investigations similar to those of English, French, and German historians are under way in other countries.

The position held by the history of fighting men within the field of military history was affirmed in August 1970 by the International Congress of Military History held in Moscow, whose theme was "*Vie et psychologie des militaires de tous grades et des partisans*" (Life and psychology of military men of all ranks, and of partisans). It was further clarified by the Colloquium on Military History held in Montpellier in September 1974 on the theme "*Recrutement, mentalité, société.*" These two conventions accorded a prominent place to the ancien regime.

The regeneration of military history has not taken place in a vacuum. It is due largely to academic scholars and to the reception given them by leading military figures, aware of the need to move away from "battle history." "Economic and social history," "institutional and social history," the study of attitudes, quantitative methods—all of which have enlivened historical research in the universities—have favored the historical analysis of armed forces and have been of great importance in the renewed interest in military history. At the same time military history seems at present to be emerging from the isolation in which it was once held by university scholars, especially in France since the period between the two world wars.

Without claiming greater importance for military events than they warrant, we must recognize that they have a strong influence not only on national activity and the growth of the State but equally on the economic, social, and mental structures of the whole of society. This is no less true for the ancien regime than for other periods. These disparate elements are closely bound together, and the role of the military event in the nation and in the State constitutes an essential element in the study of its role in society, however diverse the actual relationships between army and society may be according to period or country.

One final word. At this time documentation concerning the issues raised here is still very uneven, in value and accessibility. It consists of recent syntheses, various "problem-oriented" articles or monographs, works that are out of date but not replaced, even—for the most-neglected countries—the most general historical accounts. In such a situation an overall study may seem a little premature. It would have been easier to assess our knowledge of the issues country by country; such an approach would not be without usefulness. The bibliography at the end of this work attempts to make further investigation possible for those who wish to look for material concerning a particular country. But it has seemed to me that military history—as the ambitious title of a fairly recent work, *Histoire universelle des armées* (see Bibliography), emphasizes—can no more than religious or economic history be allowed to remain locked within a national framework. An effective innovation in the organization of armies does not often remain the exclusive property of a single country; a victorious leader usually gives rise to imitators. Thus an overview permits us to bring out the common characteristics as well as the different aspects that a military circumstance assumes, according to the make-up of each society. It is hoped that this general view will at least help scholars avoid inaccurate clichés and engage directly in the study of issues which are not yet thoroughly understood.

ACKNOWLEDGMENTS

I wish to acknowledge my indebtedness to Professor Robin Higham of Kansas State University for the friendly suggestion to which I owe this American edition of my book. Acknowledgment is due also to the Presses Universitaires de France for permission to publish this edition, and to Indiana University Press for publishing it.

I am grateful, too, to my friends Professor Claude Sturgill of the University of Florida, a fellow-researcher in the Archives de la Guerre in Paris, who has taken a helpful interest in this book and in its American edition, and Col. Bengt Ahslund, president of the Commission Internationale d'Histoire Militaire, who has corrected some errors in my discussion of the Swedish army.

An important contribution to this edition was made by Abigail Siddall, who carried out the difficult task of translating a work intended primarily for French scholars, and who caught and corrected imperfections in the first edition.

Finally, I wish to dedicate this American edition of my French text to my wife.

Paris, France   ANDRÉ CORVISIER

ARMIES
AND SOCIETIES
IN EUROPE,
1494–1789

PART I

The Nation and the Army

The simple conquest of one nation by another brings about the extreme case of a juxtaposition—or rather, a superposition—of an army and a society having no bonds with each other. The widespread military occupations during the wars of the twentieth century come to mind as examples of this. In some cases occupying forces have equipped auxiliary forces recruited from the occupied nations, although usually for only brief periods. The most characteristic example of a situation in which army and people had no ties, and the one that lasted the longest, is to be found in China from 1644 to 1911; there a Manchu army supported a ruling foreign dynasty, while the Army of the Green Banner, a kind of local Chinese militia, had no effective military structure. The case of the Ottoman Empire, which will be discussed later, is more complex. Elsewhere some interconnections are usually to be found.

It is reasonable to consider that nations existed in Europe at the beginning of the modern period, even though the conception of nationality was not precisely that which has prevailed in France since 1789. Armies existed as well, but they did not hold a monopoly in weaponry. Weapons symbolized not only the privilege and the occupation of a certain category of society, but also the right of every free individual to ensure his personal safety. It is appropriate, then, to examine first of all the role of arms in the societies of the ancien regime, before inquiring into the evolution of the idea of military obligation and military service.

1

The Place of Arms in the Societies of the Ancien Regime

SECOND ONLY to prayer, the exercise of arms was accorded the highest respect among all human activities by the societies of the ancien regime. This was not only the result of the actual situation—for in fact weapons were the instrument of power for rulers and all who were a part of the ruling society, like the feudal overlords; it was also the expression of a moral setting in which violence and respect for force characterized relationships among individuals. For this reason, an evolution in social attitudes and conceptions of life was to bring about a change in the status and role of arms in society.

ATTITUDES

At the beginning of modern times, self-control was an unreliable element. On the one hand, there existed a passiveness that resulted either from a sense of helplessness against nature and the bonds imposed by a particular station in life, or from a Christian resignation or an oriental fatalism. This did not inhibit the daily struggle for existence. On the other hand, we see evidence, particularly in eastern Europe, of an emotionalism which some-

3

times led to violent reactions and which the Christian religion could only partly control. Recourse to force was common among both peasants and city dwellers, in spite of social and moral pressures; among the nobility despite the codes of chivalry; and even on occasion among clerics. A new social order based on greater self-control did not begin to take shape until the Renaissance, when it was given expression in Italy by Balthazar Castiglione in *The Courtier*. Even then the reality often diverged widely from the theory.

The Wars of Religion and their sequels—that is, the epoque from 1560 to 1660—saw a resurgence of violence and barbarism that culminated in the Thirty Years War. In *Simplicius Simplicissimus* (1669) Grimmelshausen illustrated how difficult it was for the German people to adapt to peace. Abductions and other outrages increased, as well as the violent settling of old scores. The latter took the form among the nobility of duels, which on the whole represented an advance over murderous surprise attacks on an enemy. But even dueling, when its motives were frivolous, had the flavor of a sport, a wager, and a defiance of society and religion. Lawrence Stone has pointed out the existence of a generalized state of violence in relationships among individuals in England until about 1620. Laws forbidding dueling proliferated (in France between 1602 and 1723, in Prussia after 1669), and they eventually succeeded in limiting dueling among military personnel by creating tribunals to deal with points of honor. In France such laws were enforced by the constabulary.

All this violence took place in a general atmosphere of cruelty. The sight of blood did not bring about the same revulsion that it does today. Tournaments, outlawed in France in 1559, actually disappeared only gradually during the century with the renewal of war. Public trials by combat were still sometimes held. The French court looked on while La Châtaigneraie, wounded by Jarnac, bled to death in the arena. And there were the public executions, great spectacles that drew huge crowds and incurred almost no opposition until the abuses of the Terror. Even at the time of Louis XIV, Madame de Sévigné in 1675 described, with no evident distress, soldiers who were ordered to suppress the *Papier timbré* insurrection spitting a child on their sabres. Why should it be surprising that the massacres of Saint Bartholomew, in which corpses were dragged through the streets and thrown into the Seine, were possible and even applauded, and that it was not only the lowest orders of society who carried out these acts? Incidentally it was the fact that they resulted from the king's own order that gave these particular events notoriety; on a local scale, except in Paris, such acts were not uncommon wherever the religions came into conflict.

Above all it must not be imagined that violence was limited to brutal, hardened soldiers. Undeniably armies, friendly or foreign, often looted and burned, and soldiers stole. Such behavior was sometimes even sanctioned by the laws of warfare. Thus any town that refused to surrender could be sacked for three days after it was taken by force; an example was the sacking of Magdeburg in 1631. Or simply failure to pay troops regularly would loose them on the civilians; for example, in the sack of Rome carried out in 1527 by the armies of Charles V under the command of the Duc de Bourbon. And recourse was had often to the *dégât*, complete devastation or "scorched earth" tactics. The devastation of the Palatinate by French armies in 1689 is remembered east of the Rhine primarily because of its systematic execution and the scale on which it was carried out. Bavaria was no less cruelly ravaged by Imperial troops in 1704. The routes usually followed by the armies were areas of violence and fear despite the organization of regular supply depots. In Germany during the Thirty Years War these routes formed the axes of a "geography of destruction" (Gunther Franz). But inversely, an isolated soldier was in danger, especially if he belonged to a retreating army. Peasants would take vengeance on him for all the pain they had endured, or simply for the terror they had undergone. Their rulers had little difficulty in persuading them to pursue enemy soldiers. By the eighteenth century, however, the horrors of war tended to center on the field of combat.

Central and eastern Europe were not free of similar atrocities. The Northern War and the Austro-Turkish wars left scars. Hungary was pillaged by underpaid Imperial troops. It appears that the cruelty lasted even longer in these areas. It is in this part of Europe, incidentally, that Voltaire in the eighteenth century located the military exploits of his hero Candide. Turks and Russians especially conducted pitiless wars. Often cited is the instance of Russian soldiers who two days after the capture of Otchakov in 1788 amused themselves by tossing children from the ramparts, while their comrades caught them below on the points of their bayonets. It is less well established that civilians in the East, like those in central Europe, carried out cruel reprisals against the soldiers when they had the opportunity. But would the magnitude of the massacres, combined with a certain fatalism, always be enough to dissuade them?

MILITARY PERMEATION OF SOCIETY

The Ottoman Empire, which in some ways presents analogies with China, can be treated as a special case. On the one hand, there were the foreign conquerors, masters by military force, forbidden by their Islamic religion to assimilate with the subjugated Christians but allowed to receive Christian renegades into their ranks; on the other hand were the *raias*, those conquered peoples whom the Ottoman State allowed to administer themselves in exchange for submission and payment of tribute. In these situations military functions were clearly separated from other duties. Military leaders were granted financial subsistence for as long as they lived. The men, for example the janissaries of the sultan's guard, who were frequently taken as children from Christian families and raised as Moslems, were turned into fanatics and freed from all material cares. Little contact was allowed, theoretically, between the garrisons and the civilian populations, and it is not surprising that the effects of one on the other were slight, other than at the highest levels. This picture is probably not entirely accurate for Hungary and Transylvania, where a powerful landed aristocracy survived.

European society not affected by Islamic influence was both Christian and military at the same time. The clergy of the twelfth century had taught as part of the divine plan the idea of a three-way division of society: those who prayed, those who fought, and those who worked. This conception eventually found its way into the political institutions of the governments and became well entrenched in social institutions. Most of the Christian societies were composed of different numbers of "orders" that permitted a separation of the clergy and the nobility from the "people." Noblemen were destined primarily for the profession of arms and for positions of command. They depended on the labor of the peasants for their support, and in return they were obliged to undertake military service, that is, to pay the *impôt du sang*.

Reality is often different from the social ideal. Nobility and the profession of arms never actually coincided exactly. For one thing, the nobility, besides warriors and knights—men devoted to arms—included a growing number of magistrates and administrators in the service of the State, or simply gentlemen who, like the Sire de Gouberville, were content to look after their own estates. On the other hand, the nobility had never had a monopoly in military matters. When called by the *seigneur*, the community authorities, or later by the king, every adult male had to help defend the village, the province, or the nation. This obligation was apparently so imperative that even ecclesiastics were found participating in the struggle, although they were exempt from military service either as a matter of principle or, in some countries, by the payment of taxes. (We are not speaking here of the sixteenth-century Wars of Religion.) In Dole, besieged by the French army in 1636, a Capuchin monk served in the artillery, and Carmelites and Dominicans worked on the defensive earthworks. In France, whenever it was deemed necessary, all levels of vassals could be called up until the end of the seventeenth century—not only the *arrière-ban* of the nobility but also the various militias of the towns, frontier provinces, and coastal areas. Their ineffectiveness forced the discontinuation of such drafts, but the State made use of the principle in working out modern forms of military service.

It is tempting to make generalizations for the entire period of the ancien regime, and for all countries, based on facts observed in specific areas at certain moments—for example, during civil wars. That would lead to false impressions. But it seems equally misleading to ignore military elements in urban or rural life, as many social historians do under the false assumption that the common people engaged in no military activity. According to a rough estimate that I have put forth elsewhere, one Frenchman out of six, at the end of the reign of Louis XIV, would very likely have been called to arms at least once in his life, although not necessarily to engage in actual fighting. This figure is either low or high, according to one's point of view, but it nevertheless indicates clearly that in times of danger peaceful peasants were ready to take up arms and willing to put aside their customary lack of military ardor.

Men were called up to fight off anything that could endanger the community, not only a foreign enemy but outlaws, wolves, or—by organizing quarantine zones—epidemics. Such mobilizations probably reached their peak in the period from 1560 to 1660. Most of the time an appeal to arms was not necessary—at least until the monarchical structures raised by Louis XIV and his imitators organized forces for maintaining order, like watch companies or mounted constabulary—for until then the common man as well as the nobleman relied first on himself and his own weapons to ensure his safety, rather than on military forces of order. And to some extent throughout the ancien regime the governments left the maintenance of order to the citizens. If bearing arms was a noble privilege, it was nevertheless acknowledged that everyone could possess weapons for self-defense. Travelers were allowed to carry light arms. When one did not have an acknowledged right to bear arms, the possession of a weapon was a sign of independence. Wearing a sword distinguished the gentleman in principle, but it was allowed for many others, for example, the middle-class burghers (bourgeois) of Paris. In the eighteenth century, swords were even rented at the gates of the park of Versailles to anyone who wanted to walk there, as long as he was properly dressed.

Weapons were present everywhere: distributed during musters and for various reasons not always returned; stolen from town or State arsenals or from military personnel, and sold illegally, often disassembled; patched together from parts available in open markets like that at Beaucaire, for example. In the eighteenth century, particularly under the Regency [1715–1723], the French monarchs tried in vain to take all arms from civilians. Actually the effort was not entirely without effect. The weapons that had been openly displayed in the seventeenth century went underground in the eighteenth. In any case they were a miscellaneous collection of little military use. Indeed, simply the evolution of the military arts was removing from such light arms some of their threat to public order. The value placed on them in the second half of the eighteenth century was largely due to the defense of hunting rights on the part of the aristocracy. They would appear again during the Terror.

In the eighteenth century the French still loved gunpowder. Public ceremonies offered volleys fired by the *soldats de bourgeoisie*, and in the villages, too, guns were fired during weddings. At the time of the Revolution the refrain of "La Carma-

gnole," "*Vive le son du canon,*" expressed this taste for gunpowder. It does not appear that Frenchmen were unusual in this
respect in Europe.

The general approval of arms led to popular respect for those
who used them. Every armed assembly needs a leader. When the
gathering is spontaneous—for defense against an exterior threat,
for resistance to authority, for revolt—men begin immediately to
seek out a leader, and it was natural to think first of the nobility,
preferably of local *seigneurs*. This was true in France from the
uprising of the *Nu-pieds* in the seventeenth century to the wars of
the Vendée after the Revolution. In the absence of any aristocracy, the group would be led by a former soldier like Stofflet. The
high degree of respect for arms explains the identification that
was made in the public mind between the pursuit of arms and
aristocracy—an identification acknowledged, particularly in
France, by all those who entered the ranks of the aristocracy by
other means than the exercise of arms. Thus in Christian
Europe, in the sixteenth and seventeenth centuries at least,
society was strongly permeated with a military spirit.

Equally so was the State. Military power continued to be the
prerogative of the sovereign, even when this was a collective
being, a free city under the Empire, a Swiss canton, or the States
General of the United Provinces. In the latter country, the military governors (stadholders) could not in spite of all efforts seize
the sovereignty. Rulers often appeared on the field of battle, if
they did not actually command their own armies. Even in the
Dutch army, notably at the battle of Malplaquet (1709), a deputy
from the States General was to be found preparing his report on
the progress of military operations. And in the provinces and
towns the representative of the sovereign, the governor, was always a military person, although in France his actual powers only
covered part of the administration of the province or town.

The ancien regime, then, was filled with a military spirit, even
when the actual concerns of the citizens in provinces untouched

by war were far removed from the army. The social values were military values, and the exemplary act was, even up to the early sixteenth century, one of chivalry. It will of course be recognized that the novels of chivalry constituted a literature of "escape" that harked back to a world no longer in existence. But if chivalry had died well before Cervantes' *Don Quixote* appeared, its ethic had not entirely disappeared.

Moreover, it would be impossible to apply our present distinction between civilians and soldiers to the sixteenth and seventeenth centuries. In this sense these terms do not appear until the end of the eighteenth century. For a long time the only distinctions were between robe and sword, on the social level, and between *robe longue* (judicial function) and *robe courte* (military function) on the professional level. In many areas the "civil" and the "military" overlapped.

Thus the knights of the Middle Ages, or the townsmen or peasants called to arms, were not exactly soldiers. They were fighters, the first by vocation, the others on demand. It was the distribution of pay and above all the institution of permanent armies that gave rise to the mercenaries and to a class of men who spent the greater part of their lives in the profession of arms. Until then an officer, who was not formally enrolled, was often absent from camp, and there even existed among the troops men called volunteers, amateur soldiers without contract or wages who left whenever they wished. Many military men lived with their families, often far from the armies. On the other hand, when rulers organized permanent armies, they turned particularly to magistrates and to financiers, and the administration of the army was therefore for a long time in the hands of "civilians." It became military only at the end of the seventeenth century: under Charles XI in Sweden; under Frederick William I (the *Roi-Sergent*) in Prussia in 1721; and in Austria under Prince Eugene and especially with the reforms of Haugwitz, chancellor under Maria Theresa. In France the presence of Marshal de

Villars on the War Council from 1715 to 1718 is not an indication of a true transformation in the attitude of the war offices; that would await the reforms of Belle-Isle and Choiseul. In 1758 Belle-Isle was the first military man appointed secretary of state for war. All these changes are symbolic, revealing the fact that the position of the army in the State and in society was undergoing a transformation.

THE NEW POSITION OF ARMS IN EIGHTEENTH-CENTURY SOCIETY

The manner of this evolution was not uniform throughout Europe. In some countries—Italy, the United Provinces, England, France, Spain—it was manifested by a generally lowered esteem for arms on the part of the general public. In contrast, in Sweden, Prussia, Russia, and even in the Hapsburg monarchy, the army became on the whole more firmly established as one of the moral as well as material supports of the monarch, although there were of course differences from one country to another. In general, except in Prussia, the distinction between civil and military became more clear-cut, with pre-eminence assigned to the former in western Europe, to the latter in the East. A case apart is Poland, where the disintegration of the national army led to the fragmentation of the State.

Was the Renaissance of literature and art inimical to the military spirit? I think not. In Italy the Renaissance favored the study of the military arts, ballistics, and fortification, as of all areas of knowledge. Throughout western Europe it helped to endow the national spirit with historic justification, exalting heroes, like Vercingetorix and Arminius, who had opposed the Roman conquest. Its cartographic advances clarified the idea of the frontier, and it spawned academies where young noblemen learned the exercise of arms. Nevertheless, particularly in the sixteenth century although somewhat in the fifteenth as well, the value of many temporal activities besides arms was being asserted. Admittedly it was a rare merchant, artist, or humanist (other than clerics within and outside the universities) who had not at some time held a sword; but the military spirit clearly did not dominate their characters. Concern with arms encountered a powerful concurrent force in public esteem, that of money. This is not the place to discuss how the condemnations of money—repeated vehemently by the mendicant orders in preceding centuries— were now modified, not only in Calvinist Europe but in all places where economic activity was moving energetically forward. And with the advances in military technique money had become as indispensable in the make-up of modern armies as the latter were in the defense of economic activities.

It was in Italy that a reduction in the popularity of arms began, as the jurist, the writer, and the artist rose to prominence in society. By the time of Charles V, the era of the *condottieri*, who had been relied upon to defend the State, was over; the Spanish army took over the charge. The people no longer contributed to defense other than with tax money. Venice still had an army, but it was used primarily to protect colonial possessions from the Turks. Florence and the Church States had only a few troops composed of mercenaries, often foreign. City militias became increasingly police forces. Armies became foreign to the country, and Italians who had ambition and were attracted to a military career went off to serve in Spain, France, or Germany. Piedmont was an exception (and is discussed below).

In the United Provinces and in England, economic activity overtook the military. In Holland at the end of the Eighty Years War against Spain, during which the stadholders and the army had played an important political role, the return of peace led to the suppression of the stadholders and the subordination of the army to the civil power (1650). For twenty-two years Holland took practically no measures for defense. In 1672, following invasion, the stadholder system was re-established, but the reorganized army was raised by the States General. In England the military regime of the Protectorate collapsed in 1659, leaving an unfavorable memory. The restored king had no permanent army other than his own guard and a few units. The formation of a new army, carried out discreetly by Charles II and more openly by James II, was condemned by the "Glorious Revolution" of 1688; the king could no longer raise troops without the consent of Parliament.

These political events accompanied a more basic evolution. First of all, it was no coincidence that a reduction in military pervasiveness took place in two countries that faced the sea, and in which large money fortunes were being accumulated. Further, in England the boundaries between nobility and middle class were much more flexible than on the continent. Acquiring noble rank was fairly easy, and gentlemen did not scorn mercantile activity. The heart of the United Provinces consisted of the maritime provinces of Holland and Zeeland, in which almost half the population were town dwellers, and where the nobility had only a limited role. The outstanding prosperity of the United Provinces and that which was developing in England in the seventeenth century explain this reversal of values. It can be considered thoroughly established by the early eighteenth century, when Addison and Steele, in the *Spectator* and the *Tatler*, scoffed at the customs and tastes of the hereditary nobility: "A skillful merchant is the best kind of gentleman in the nation." Scarcely ever threatened on their own soil in the early 1700s, these two nations allowed their armies to become weak. The English army was to become variable in size, limited in peacetime, composed primarily of mercenaries from the continent, intended largely for operations outside the country; it remained somewhat on the margins of society, except of course for the officers. The situation was similar in the United Provinces.

France, where the army was firmly in the hands of the king (*ordonnance* of 1583), especially after the failure of the Fronde, underwent an evolution similar to that of the maritime powers, but nearly a century later. There are many reasons for the delay. First, we must remember that from 1521 to 1659 the kingdom was menaced by the invasions that were ravaging Picardy, Champagne, Burgundy, the Dauphiné, and Provence. Because of the civil wars the interior provinces were crisscrossed by armies, often made up of foreigners. Paris underwent several threats (1544, 1591—when it acquired a Spanish garrison—1636) and several sieges (1589, 1591, 1594, 1648, 1652). It was not until the reign of Louis XIV, with its annexations and Vauban's organization of the "iron frontier," that France knew security. So it is not surprising that seventeenth-century Frenchmen maintained their preoccupation with military matters, and that the city militias held—until the Fronde—a not unimportant military position.

The treaties of Utrecht and Rastatt [in 1713 and 1714] introduced a new period. Frontier provinces, often recently annexed, and some neighboring regions were assigned a military role, but the "interior" withdrew from military activities, which no longer meant anything more than increased taxes and the raising of the unpopular royal militia created by Louvois, to be sent to wars that were for the most part outside the country. This partitioning of the kingdom was clearly evident in the division of provincial correspondence between the war secretariat for the frontier provinces, and the Royal Household, which was gradually being transformed into an Interior Ministry. And again, the wars of Louis XIV, to which were attributed the widespread famine and mortality of 1694 and 1709, left unfavorable memories.

Other attitudes were changing at the time, and after 1680 new social concepts evolved. Religious, political, and social institutions were subjected to the criticism of reason, and the idea of progress was making headway. Restoration of relations with England in 1713 reinforced the trend. The Regency witnessed the imperious domination of money as a human preoccupation, and, with the Enlightenment, the aristocrat and the military man ceded the highest place in the scale of social values to the thinkers, scholars, and producers working for the temporal happiness of mankind. For many, military affairs had to bow before economic activity. We even see Fontette, the provincial administrator of Caen—a region threatened by England, after all—declare that a few small raids by the English would do no more harm to Normandy than would the preparations for its defense.

Developments in Portugal, Spain, and Piedmont followed the same trend. Portugal, its independence assured by the outcome of a long war (1640–1664), was primarily interested in maritime affairs. Spain had possessed, supported, and kept in training the most powerful army of its time in the sixteenth and early seventeenth centuries. Despite the presence at the court of many men of letters, the military under Philip II gained an importance all the greater in that a good share of the external trade had fallen into the hands of foreigners. The popular *picaro* in literature, the hero of the "picaresque" novel, does not have a military character, but he is nevertheless a man accustomed to using weapons. We must remember, too, that it was within the Spanish aristocracy that the code of honor practiced by gentlemen of western Europe in the seventeenth century had taken shape, and that the duel was its favored means of settling disputes. Nevertheless in the seventeenth century the formidable "Spanish infantry" included only a minority of Spaniards, about 15 percent. Military activity had involved all townsmen and peasants, but militias now fell into disorder. The invasion of 1706–1711 revealed the strength of national sentiment, but it did not turn Spain into a military nation. In the eighteenth century the recurring Iberian Wars (1704–1713, 1719, 1739–1748, 1756–1763) only intensified the enmity between Portugal—now an English base—and Spain. In fact Spain was becoming incorporated into a wider European perspective. The Pyrenees frontier was hardly disturbed except in 1719. Reforming ministers, even the bellicose

Alberoni, sought ways to reorganize administration and stimulate the economy, and if their advice was not always followed by the Spanish it does not appear to be because of nostalgia for warfare and military glory.

As for Piedmont, it took part in all the wars and often served as a battlefield. Its rulers tried to nourish a military vocation among their subjects, even organizing a royal militia on the French model. But military affairs did not hold an important place in the concerns and lives of the people, as they did in Prussia at the time.

Outside western Europe the scene is different. Poland was a special case. Surrounded by enemies and without clear frontiers—at least on the east—this country experienced both wars of conquest and invasions. For many of the *szlachta*, the petty nobility who served the king or other princes, war was the principal activity. The common people shared this military spirit: townsmen undertook to defend their towns, and peasants—armed by their lords—were equally ready to take up arms at any sign of danger from Turkish "infidels" or German or Russian "heretics." And in the eighteenth century, threats from abroad were usually found to be supported by internal factions that were tearing the country apart. Violating the decisions of the Diet, several armed confederations were formed, eventually bringing about the ruin of State and army in the "Republic of Poland."

On the eastern borders of Poland military republics had been established. These Cossack states united groups of peasant soldiers who had managed to escape from the authority of the Polish government, which they had undertaken to protect against the Turks. With a political center—the *setch* of elected chiefs (atamans or hetmans)—and a warrior ethic, these Cossack groups joined together, sometimes fought one another, multiplied with the help of the Russian government, and moved eastward from the Dnieper to the Don and then to the Urals. They had a distinct influence on the art of warfare in central Europe (especially on cavalry), but it is difficult to see any imitation of their structure in the Swedish, Prussian, and Russian military reforms.

In the seventeenth and eighteenth centuries certain of Poland's neighbors, unfortunately for her, became military states. An example is Sweden under Gustavus Adolphus. In this extensive country, where a scattered population struggled within a difficult natural setting, Gustavus Adolphus reorganized some old militias into a small permanent national army inspired with a crusading zeal. Actually these recruits were only a small part of the Swedish army, but the example was to be picked up by Charles XI in the system of the *Indelningsverket*, whose organization we will examine fully later. The country was divided into cantons corresponding to the recruitment area for a regiment. This system allowed the use of and familiarity with weapons to penetrate throughout the country, and it was in its turn to inspire Prussian and Russian rulers.

The organization of the Prussian military State was initiated by the Great Elector [Frederick William of Brandenburg, d. 1688] with the creation over his separate territories of a general war commissariat having in its province all matters touching the army directly or indirectly. It was concluded by Frederick William I, who announced in an edict in 1714 shortly after his accession that "young men, according to their natural condition and by the order of the Highest, must serve with their possessions and with their blood." His director of Finances, Wars, and Domains (1721) subordinated administrative activity to the interests of the army, which continued to receive support from his successors as well. By the will of the sovereign, the nobility was required to serve the State permanently, for the most part in the army. After 1731 the *Kantonsystem*, modeled on the Swedish system, forced all fit men in the nation to become soldiers. Enrolled at the age of ten, they had to undertake military training for two years at the age of twenty, then serve to whatever extent they could during several months each year. A Prussian people quite different from other Germans emerged from this, strongly characterized by a military spirit. The landed gentry practiced on their estates the military discipline that they were used to exerting over the men in their companies when training them for service. Soldiers while at home on leave had to wear part of their uniforms, and the peasants often wore old uniforms that the army passed down to them.

The Swedish and Prussian models were copied in an old nation, Russia. It was of course impossible to militarize this immense, thinly populated country, and to impose on its diverse peoples a canton system as strict as the Prussian one. But from the time of Peter the Great, the State and its administration took on a military aspect which won over the Russian aristocracy. All servants of the State, members of the nobility at all levels (*tchine*), civil administrators as well as military officers, were subject to the same military discipline, and at the end of the eighteenth century they were obliged to wear uniforms. Military values were well established in the ethic of the aristocracy and in the attitudes of the Russian State.

The case of the Hapsburg monarchy is obviously more complex. The Bohemian peoples were disarmed after the battle of White Mountain (1620), but danger from the Turks kept military concern alive in Austria at least until the battle of Kahlenberg (1683), and the country underwent fairly long periods of warfare until 1763. Hungary was in some ways similar to Poland, in that the State became firmly established while at the same time an important role was granted to the aristocracy. On the eastern borders *confins militaires* were organized; they were inhabited by peasant-soldiers, and their administration was purely military. On the other hand, by the eighteenth century the attitude of the peoples in the Hereditary States resembled that in the other German states except for Prussia. After the treaties of Westphalia in 1648 a distinct lessening of the military spirit was evident in the minor German states; Germans who wanted a military career took service in Austrian, Prussian, French, Dutch, English, or Russian armies. This became less true in the eighteenth century, when rulers of the central states organized armies and even militias according to the French model. Some small principalities put their entire force at the service of foreign powers. Bavaria's situation resembled that of Piedmont to some extent. Emperor Leopold and Prince Eugene were the true creators of the modern Austrian army. After the War of the Austrian Succession in 1740–1741 the Hapsburgs, attracted by the Prussian example, attempted to give a more military aspect to their states.

Thus, in the middle of the eighteenth century, militarily constituted nations and nations where respect for arms was receding faced each other in Europe. If the philosophy of the Enlightenment played a part in the lowered esteem for arms in western Europe, in central and eastern Europe those rulers who were inspired by the Enlightenment tried to create a military framework that called for a still greater respect for arms. We must take into account this difference in the values upon which government and society were based, in order to understand European conceptions of military duty and military service.

2

Military Duty in
Times of Danger

EXCEPT IN areas controlled by foreign military troops, few citizens refused to bear arms in their own defense in times of extreme peril. After the Middle Ages men were called upon fairly often to take part in defense and to help maintain public order. Admittedly such participation did not always mean personal service; often it took the form of supplying and supporting fighting men or paying fees specifically for the maintenance of armed forces. But in extreme cases personal service was required even from those who had bought themselves off in such ways, for example, in besieged towns or in France in 1814 and 1870.

The concept of military duty, however, has undergone a long and complicated evolution. We must look first at the motivations that made military service acceptable to those who had no interest in military careers, then at the different forms such service took, and finally at the elements of early forms of military service that survived into the seventeenth and eighteenth centuries.

MOTIVATION

The strongest and most consistent motivation was the defense of family, property, and land against invaders. This concern can readily be extended to include the goods of neighbors, and it is

21

this sentiment that is expressed in certain words of "La Marseillaise." It is the attachment to the fatherland, to use the term in its basic meaning—the land of one's forefathers. The fatherland took on varying dimensions. Originally the village, the local working group, or the rural estate, it quickly spread outwards, according to the natural tendency of any group to push back the limits of danger and surround itself with others with whom its members can live peacefully. Conversely, fear or simply the inconvenience of ties to a larger geographical unit sometimes led to isolationism. As late as the nineteenth century certain small communities in the Massif Central evaded military registration and service, for their patriotism meant an attachment only to their individual hamlets and they felt little community of interest with their neighbors. This sentiment explains, too, the city dwellers who, despite important economic connections between towns and surrounding agricultural areas, willingly sacrificed the countryside to defend their cities.

The area included in one's sense of community and thus unity in the face of danger corresponds to the degree of knowledge of the world. It varied among individuals according to their activities, their levels of education, and their social positions. The optimum extension of this basic patriotism was the *pays*, the "native land"—in Germany the *Gau*—often a small geographical unit no larger than the area that could be crossed on foot in one day, and in which a common way of life prevailed; it frequently corresponded to the zone of influence of a middle-sized town. Even when the large states were formed, the feeling that each *pays* should defend itself remained. This is the reason for all the local militias that we encounter in Switzerland, in England, or among the American colonists, as well as in the Vendée, where many deserted from the royalist Catholic army as soon as it moved away from the region. For example, "the men of Ancenis" considered that it was up to "the men of Savenay" to take over if military activity turned in that direction.

Those who were the readiest to enlarge the territorial frame of the fatherland were those who studied or traveled. The clerics of the High Middle Ages, in maintaining among the faithful an awareness of the institution of royalty (which was otherwise seldom evident), ensured the continued existence of a superior community, the kingdom, within the heart of the Christian world. There is no other way to explain the fact that in eleventh-century France, which was divided into small feudal units, a mediocre king was able to arouse a response, however feeble it may have been, by raising his standard at Saint Denis for reasons clear only to those who were actually under German attack. Wars and a general distrust of foreigners helped to extend the concept of the fatherland to the States as they were formed, and to give rise to the idea of a nation symbolized by the king. (Whether the king ever completely embodied the national ideal is doubtful.) It can be claimed that the French and English nations were firmly established during the wars in which they opposed each other, and similar instances can be found elsewhere.

The concept of the nation was, of course, less precise in the sixteenth century than it has been since the end of the eighteenth century. We know that provinces changed hands by transfer of sovereignty through inheritance or grants. The people on the whole accepted any arrangement if their own institutions or their ties with the neighboring *pays* were unchanged. By not taking this sentiment into account Philip II provoked revolt in the Low Countries. In contrast, the astute Francis I could rely on the protests of the Parlement of Paris and the Burgundy states in his refusal to carry out the order imposed by the treaty of Madrid to cede Burgundy. It was not simply a matter of playing a game; the inhabitants in fact feared to be cut off from the French kingdom. Later, the Germans did not really feel they had lost Alsace until Louis XIV made a French province of it, thirty years after the rights to it had been ceded to the king of France.

Inheritances and marriages sometimes led to the establishment of a foreign dynasty, except in France. The Empire under Charles V showed that attachment to a sovereign of foreign origin was not incompatible with national sentiment. It was necessary, however, for Charles to appear Flemish in Flanders, Castilian in Castile, Neapolitan in Naples, and so on, and for him to allow natives to govern in each country. Several states, however, permitted no foreign sovereign to rule: France, with its Salic law, and the Empire, where only a German had any chance of being elected emperor. (Francis of Lorraine, elected emperor in the eighteenth century, was already a prince of the Empire.) England accepted foreign princes in 1689 and 1714, but not without imposing guaranties which made it clear that the king no longer had complete sovereignty. And in all the monarchies foreign queens were likely to be frowned upon.

As the concept of Christian unity grew weaker, and as pressure grew during the Renaissance for a common language within each country, the foundations of the nations were established. New translations of the Bible into vernacular languages played a part in this, as did the dropping of Latin in legislative and judicial transactions (in France, following the *ordonnance* of Villers-Cotterêts, 1539). The humanists insisted, too, on a common regional past, which they accordingly formulated. Primarily from certain passages in Caesar's *Commentaries* they constructed a pattern of national temperaments. All of this passed gradually into the minds of the public, especially those on the margins of the languages and cultures. Populations always tend to see themselves as different from one another, each group considering itself to be without the faults that facile stereotypes ascribe to others.

Opposing these tendencies were the savagery of the Wars of Religion and the actions that appeared to repudiate any national feeling. Yet no one would claim that the violent ideological conflicts of the revolutionary epoch or of our own time signify an absence of national sentiment. Appealing to a foreign leader to free a nation from a yoke judged to be intolerable is a tempting if unusual course, particularly in a unified state; the war between the Spanish and the English carried out on French soil at the end of the sixteenth century bears some resemblance to more recent events.

The national monarchies from the time of Louis XIV on, the progress in education, and to a lesser extent the mingling brought about by the institution of royal militias in the eighteenth century contributed to the reinforcement of national sentiment, to the point that by 1789 the survival of provincial and local privileges had become unacceptable to the French. In Europe in general, especially by the time of "enlightened despotism," progress was being made toward making local administration, within the framework of the central governments, simpler and more uniform. A sense of national solidarity in the face of foreign opposition was evident in times of war. One concrete sign of the attachment to the national idea is the fact that men in service made of their uniforms—never before looked upon as a livery— the symbol of their nationality. The Redcoats or the *Culs blancs* became an element of national identity. And in all armies it became increasingly difficult to enlist foreign units. At the end of the eighteenth century, Frenchmen served less often abroad and Germans enlisted more reluctantly in non-German armies. The German regiments in the French army included more and more German-speaking men from Alsace and Lorraine.

EARLY FORMS OF MILITARY SERVICE

The barbarian invasions of the Roman Empire revived the practice of requiring military service from all free men, a policy that the Pax Romana had made unnecessary by entrusting the defense of the empire to professional armies. The dissolution of the Carolingian empire was accompanied by a scattering of the armies, and each *seigneur* had, or tried to have, armed followers. Carolingian capitulary ordinances fixed the military obligations of free men in proportion to their landholdings: a small manor had to furnish one completely equipped knight. The *champ de mai* was a regular or occasional gathering of all men obliged to serve, called up by royal proclamation and placed in groups under the command of the counts. According to the *jus sequellae*, or in German areas *Heerfolge*, citizens had to leave their homes to join the king's army; it was an obligation that took precedence over the *Landfolge*, or the duty to defend one's own region. The independence of the great landowning counts threatened these assemblies, and the terms of the *service d'ost* officially authorized the assignment of the armed contingents to the feudal lords (*Gerichtfolge*). The formation of large, well-organized fiefs led to the creation of armies made up of vassals, and when the term of active duty was fixed at forty days a year it became customary to pay those kept on beyond this specified time. The use of mercenaries reappeared, at first in the form of granting *fiefs de soudée* (estates held by service) in the Holy Land; later, companies were formed whose leaders hired them out for the best offer. In the feudal monarchies the sovereign followed the same practices, and as towns grew powerful one of the signs of their independence was the right to form militias to ensure order and protection.

The king lost control of the organizing of troops in his kingdom, but he did not give up the right of calling men to active duty, which he continued to assert more or less successfully; at the king's call, fiefs and communities had to bring out their troops. French historians have emphasized the importance of the Battle of Bouvines (1214) and the role played in it by the contingents from the communes, or free towns. The entire body of the vassals and their vassals in turn represented a national army, in principle. The expression *"ban et arrière-ban"* was limited to knights and their servitors, but like Philippe Contamine [see Bibliography] we can speak of a "general *arrière-ban*" when the call-up included the town reserves as well. It was as close to a general mobilization as one can imagine for the fourteenth century.

In the Germanic countries, the *Heerfolge* disappeared, while the *Landfolge* and the *Gerichtfolge* survived. Imperial ordinances of 1485, 1555, and 1654 reminded the bourgeois of their obligations to defend their towns. In Hungary the *seigneurs* took over the military organizing of the population, and their troops, the *banderia*, constituted the "rising of the nobility," that is, the *arrière-ban*. Actually a call-up seldom involved an entire kingdom but only the provinces next to the threatened regions.

In the seventeenth century, rulers still sometimes ordered their subjects to attack pillaging enemy soldiers without mercy, for example, the Swedish soldiers in Upper Swabia in 1631, or Spanish and Imperial troops in France in 1636. Except for these unusual instances, the general *arrière-ban* excluded the masses, who had no military structure. At the end of the fifteenth century attempts were made to draw particular individuals from this group to form a more or less permanent army. But the *arrière-ban* was still limited to the nobility, or to owners of fiefs, whenever they were not already in service. In France it was regulated by numerous *ordonnances*. Proclaimed fairly often, it lost all military value when aristocrats who sought military careers were almost entirely absorbed by the armies under the great officers of Louis XIV, as the art of warfare became more complex. It is often asserted that the *arrière-ban* was not repeated after 1695; in fact it was seen again in the eighteenth century, but in a local and limited fashion, as in Normandy during the War of the Spanish Succession. In Prussia it was transformed into a tax in 1717. In order to mobilize the *roturiers* (those of non-noble birth), new institutions were required.

SURVIVAL OF EARLY FORMS OF MILITARY SERVICE IN WESTERN EUROPE

Among the various forms of traditional militias found in western Europe we can distinguish two types besides the *arrière-ban* of the nobility: urban or bourgeois militias, in which the police role became more important than the military role from the end of the seventeenth century on, and regional militias composed mostly of peasants called upon to cooperate for defense.

Here we are dealing with forms of military obligation that did not take men away from their homes—or at least not for long periods. It was a question of a duty to perform a local service for the purpose of security, against disorderly elements as well as possible foreign enemies. Reaching a peak during the sixteenth and seventeenth centuries in those countries racked by civil war, this form of service after the late 1600s was called on increasingly for tasks that were auxiliary to the army, because progress in military technology now required more extensive training. In many cases such service deteriorated badly, to the extent that in France any connection between the town militias and the national guards of the Revolution and the nineteenth century, if it exists at all, is very tenuous. Such early forms of service, however, did persist throughout Europe.

In the Hapsburg Netherlands the *arrière-ban* was invoked fairly frequently until 1759. Aristocratic companies were formed to defend threatened spots, for example, in Luxembourg. The cities possessed active militias during the Eighty Years War (1580–1660), notably major municipal artilleries with cannon companies, for war in Flanders often took the form of siege warfare. And urban militias were frequently called upon to furnish contingents for the "natural Prince of the Netherlands," as the Hapsburg monarch was called. Peasant companies as well as companies of townsmen were organized during the Eighty Years War. In Spain as well, towns possessed militias, forces of defense and order.

In all the western European countries, sovereigns made use of the military obligations of their subjects, moving gradually toward the practice of the levy, as in England in 1626, or in France in 1636. They required the provinces and towns to furnish soldiers equipped at their own expense, without specifying how the men were to be chosen. Such an approach stemmed from a fundamental notion of the ancien regime that many of the subjects' obligations were collective, that is, that the strong were to support the weak; it was simply up to the towns and provinces to provide fighting men for the country. The towns paid for volunteers, but this form of mercenary practice had nothing to do with the personal military obligation of the subjects.

During this period several efforts were made to create a regional army that would be ready in times of war to replace regular troops in the garrisons. The most successful measures were those initiated in sixteenth-century Spain. In 1495–1496 royal orders had called for a census of all male citizens and created a basis for a militia modeled on the local militias, the *Santa Hermandad*. Once established, however, the militias were losing their efficiency, and in 1516 Cardinal Cisneros, regent of Castile, commissioned Colonel Rengifo to prepare a general reorganization. Opposed to the idea of a general arming of the country for fear of popular disorder, Cisneros envisioned a militia of 31,800 men, to be given certain privileges, similar to the *francs-archers* organized in France by Charles VII (see p. 49). They would remain in their villages at the disposition of the district governors, undergoing training on Sundays and holidays. Opposition by the townsmen prevented the execution of the plan, however. In 1535 every town had to provide and support a temporary contingent of volunteers to reinforce the royal army in the conflict with France. Inaction, however, always weakened militia forces, and the rising of the Moors in Granada in 1569 found them unprepared. Philip II had to take up the matter again, and in 1590 a militia of 60,000 men, which had the character of a nationwide force, was established. The king had to promise not to send the militiamen abroad, however. Particularly interesting orders issued in 1598 arranged for levies by provinces. This militia fell into neglect in the seventeenth century but never entirely disappeared. In 1692, 465,000 men were listed in the registers, although only 59,000 were equipped with arms, some 12.7 percent. Furthermore, the responsibility was unequally distributed. While 6 percent were armed in the province of Valladolid and 4.5 percent in that city, the percentage rose to 22 percent in the frontier province of Zamora and 15 percent in the city itself. In actual practice, the provinces and towns appealed to volunteers to fill up the quotas, and it became, therefore, another instance of a collective military obligation.

The Spanish example was not unique, and the sixteenth century produced a first wave of militia formation within the frameworks of the States. At the beginning of the seventeenth century, la Bavière based his *Landesdefension* on the levying of men in proportion to the degree of danger (the "third," the "fifth," the "tenth," up to the "thirtieth"), placing them in units called territorial ensigns (*Landfahnen*). The men had to undertake active training twenty-four days a year. Such service granted certain rights as "townsmen" (*droit de bourgeoisie*) to those without such rights.

In Prussia, even after the inauguration of regular military service, military obligation persisted for peasants not in permanent units. A *Landmiliz* continued to exist on the frontiers of eastern Prussia, in Pomerania in the Brandenburg border areas, and in Magdeburg and Halberstadt. In Farther Pomerania a village frequently had to provide a night watchman to prevent desertion by soldiers and peasants.

In France it was the end of the seventeenth century before a true royal militia was instituted. French militias before the reign of Louis XIV were of various, often ill-assorted, types—town militias (*milices bourgeoises*), traditional local forces, occasional temporary militias, and the coastal guards. In the eyes of the sixteenth century these associations appeared to be the most all-encompassing basis for national defense, or as we would say, general mobilization. An interesting example is the military organization undertaken by the Protestants, which was tolerated after the Edict of Nantes [1598]: from the strongholds, or secure places, for which the town militias were the basic forces, to the broader organization of the countryside begun by Rohan in 1611, which gathered together local militias, feudal levies, and mercenaries. The failure of the Fronde temporarily put an end to the town militias as a military force, but their structure continued to exist everywhere except in Paris. As soon as they no longer presented any danger to the monarchy, Louis XIV, with the intention of making money and at the same time unifying his forces, proclaimed an edict in 1694 creating *"colonels, majors, capitains et lieutenans"* for certain cities and towns of the kingdom, positions which were then put up for sale. The edict also defined the responsibility of the militias, which was primarily to maintain public order. The burghers, however, appear to have supported the existence of the militias while only reluctantly accepting the obligations. In effect the militias meant that officers were exempted from providing lodging for soldiers, as well as from certain other responsibilities, and that the city as a whole—at least until 1742—was not required to provide men for the royal militia.

These *milices bourgeoises* did not merely march in parades at public ceremonies. They held a role that was auxiliary to the army: to guard prisoners of war and to look after new recruits. At times they furnished contingents to be sent to threatened spots in their provinces. In 1758, the men of Honfleur armed themselves at the news of an English approach. But the town militias had above all a police role, at least wherever permanent privileged companies had not been formed (companies that we can call town guards, like the *Cinquanteniers* and *Arquebusiers* of Rouen). The basic duty of all these forces was nightly rounds carried out in turn by district squads. Bordeaux had six militia regiments, each commanded by one of the six aldermen of the town and corresponding to one of six districts. Usually guard duty came around to each once a month. But the monarchy was increasing the use of guard companies as permanent police forces. There are frequent signs in the second half of the eighteenth century of reluctance to serve in the town militias. Townsmen hired substitutes at twelve sous a night; then, complaining about the need for this, they demanded the elimination of the service requirement (although not of the militias themselves) and were sometimes willing to leave to the regular troops the task of maintaining order, as in Le Havre. In ending this discussion of the *milices bourgeoises*, we should note that the municipal artillery corps in French Flanders, for example, that of Lille, lasted until the Revolution.

Regional militias present just as great a variety. At first there were none in many provinces of the interior, where there was no need for them. In other areas they were regularly levied in times of war throughout the ancien regime, according to traditional patterns. These "little militias," as they were called after the end of the seventeenth century, are illustrated particularly by the militias of Béarn, Boulogne, and Messina; they assembled in all about 15,000 men at a maximum. Other provinces had only temporary militias, whose formation was sometimes demanded by the citizens themselves in an attempt to avoid service in the royal militia, as the latter carried the risk of being transferred away from home; the monarchy organized these only in urgent cases. They are often called *milices bourgeoises*, although they were primarily rural. The best example is that of Languedoc, formed in 1685 to control a possible Protestant uprising. It encompassed fifty-two regiments of eight to twelve companies, according to the local resources, who assembled for review and training exercises. A network of routeways was created at the same time to connect the strongholds. "Although these troops," wrote Basville, the district administrator, "lack the command and discipline of regulars, they will always be better than a populace assembled hastily, with no order, no arms, and no leaders." Similar organizations were found elsewhere, like the *milices bourgeoises* of Briançon, Embrun, and Gap, intended to prevent a revolt by religious groups in case of invasion, as well as to close the route for possible deserters from the French army. On the eastern and northern frontiers, peasants were frequently armed to guard bridges and passes; the Somme was guarded in this way between 1706 and 1712. All of these incidental militias had primarily a preventive role.

Coast-guard militias carried out a preventive function as well, securing local defenses. The old *guet de mer* (sea-watch) was the earliest form, first in evidence on the Mediterranean coasts, where its task was to watch for Barbary pirates, in Spain (particularly Granada), then in England and France. In the last country, the structure of the coastal militia was outlined simply under Francis I in the early sixteenth century. Service was required from all men of sound health, from eighteen to sixty years of age, who lived in any parish whose church was less than two leagues from the coast. Responsibilities consisted of manning guardposts at elevated spots, particularly church towers, signaling by fires the approach of suspicious ships, and assembling at possible landing places to make it clear to an aggressor that he could not take the place by surprise. Louis XIV reorganized the coastal guard by forming detached companies of coast-guard soldiers, armed and regularly trained, charged with securing landing places until regular troops arrived. All other able bodied men were put into "watch" companies. Each detached company was given responsibility for a group of parishes, and the character of these coast-guard units became increasingly military during the wars between France and England.

The English militia probably offers the most highly developed illustration of early forms of required military service. This is due to the persistence of medieval practices, to the reluctance to pay taxes to support a regular army, and after 1660 to the distrust of a permanent army. Benefiting from the lack of complexity in English governmental administration, the Tudors set up a complete system based on the division of the country into counties. General musters of the militias were ordered several times in the early sixteenth century, and Henry VIII raised as many as 120,000 men in 1545. A statute proclaimed under Edward VI and in effect from 1558 until 1603 reaffirmed the military obligation of all subjects from sixteen to sixty below the rank of baron. Division was made into ten groups according to landholdings, conforming to earlier practice. A man whose income was from five to ten pounds a year had to equip himself with cuirass and helmet, if necessary with the help of others. Those with more than 1,000 pounds a year had to supply sixteen horses, eighty suits of armor, fifty helmets, twenty harquebuses, and so forth. These obligations did not always imply personal service but rather a financial obligation for all freeholders of at least five pounds' income a year.

Deputy lieutenants commanded the militias of the counties, each of which was divided into hundreds. The basic unit was the parish. The gentry provided officers, who were assisted by county inspectors, chief constables of the hundreds, constables of the towns, and churchwardens of the rural parishes; the latter kept the militia registers and were responsible for the weapons. Before 1570 the registers listed about a million names in all of England, but the number of men actually trained by muster masters (usually former soldiers) was scarcely over 100,000. Particular places of assembly, like Mile End near London, were famous.

The Catholic revolt of 1569 revealed the weakness of these forces and led Queen Elizabeth to organize this mass of men. In 1573 trained bands, whose members received pay, were created. At the time of the Spanish threat, the coastal defenses were improved to include a preventive screen along the coasts with reinforcements disposed in depth behind it. This force, on the alert from 1588 to 1598, was never put to the test of war.

It would be inaccurate to assume that this militia was organized in a uniform manner throughout the kingdom, corresponding exactly to the outlines of county administration. The City of

London and the Cinque Ports had their own militias. Many men avoided the county musters and came under the direct control of the secretary of state. First, there were those who served in place of the clergy (who were authorized to arrange for substitutes, as were university members). Then the barons could keep armed men, personal retainers, in their own service, and they themselves presided over the musters of militiamen on their estates. After 1588 the chartered towns obtained the same privilege. Thus the English forces preserved a feudal aspect, and patronage was still the practice among subalterns and noncommissioned officers in making up the units that they commanded. It was always difficult to put together mounted troops, and social distinctions were established between harquebusiers, recruited usually in the towns, and pikemen and bowmen, who were mostly peasants and paupers.

The English militia was affected by two contradictory tendencies: the traditional inclination was to keep at home the richest and most skilled men for the defense of England, and to send abroad the troops consisting of men whom the country wished to get rid of. On the other hand, many militiamen who were well off chose to avoid service by hiring substitutes from the very lowest levels of men.

In 1603 James I rescinded the statute of 1558, but he did not abandon the militia, which was, however, dormant until Charles I called on it in 1626. A new structure was planned, using many of the schemes projected during the reign of Elizabeth I. It was suggested several times that elite troops, those most effective in military action, should be drawn from the militia. But the practice of substitution caused fears of large assemblies of the armed poor. The grandiose plans for an "exact militia," or a "select militia" (1629) could not be carried out, but at least the worn-out weapons were replaced. When the Civil War began, Charles I simply put back into effect the 1558 statute.

After the execution of Charles I the militia no longer had a military role, but it quickly became apparent that it could exert considerable force in political conflicts. The "Barebones Parliament" created a militia of 6,000 volunteer horsemen. In 1660 the militia was restored along with the king and the political powers of Parliament, but it carried no obligatory service and was intended as a check on Cromwellians and Papists (declarations of 1661 and 1663). The Catholic policies of James II and the progress of toleration at the beginning of the eighteenth century dealt a severe blow to the militia, and by the middle of the century it had lost all value as a political support.

In western Europe after 1660, for military, political, and social reasons, the military obligations of the subjects, although not annulled, were less often carried out according to the old forms of military service. On the whole, citizens agreed to serve in cases of urgent danger, but military service had a new meaning. Considered from the start to be a privilege of free men, it carried with it in all countries a certain status as well as exemptions of all sorts, especially financial. The fighting role became less important as military technology progressed, and the militias were limited to more modest tasks. Armed service persisted in the area of maintaining public order, without—despite the composition of most militias—giving rise to a militia of the wealthy (as the national guards were later to be in their opposition to all threats to existing social order). In France, middle-class townsmen continued to support the militias because they carried with them certain privileges, but everywhere those bound to the old militias attempted to get out of serving personally. The *soldats de bourgeoisie* appeared mostly in parades, calling on substitutes— usually from the poorest classes—for less desirable tasks. In England and later in France there grew up a tendency to consider actual military service as the fate of only the most miserable men, and the position of the soldier (although not the officer) as one deprived of all freedom. In the century of the Enlightenment in western Europe, general opinion agreed to leave defense to permanent armies made up of professional soldiers.

EARLY FORMS OF MILITARY
SERVICE IN EASTERN EUROPE

These were usually linked with possession of the land that was awarded to an armed man to provide him a means of living—the *timar* in Turkey, *pomestié* in Russia—similar to the fiefs granted earlier in the West. Military duty existed only through a feudal system and tended to center around a landed aristocracy, not the sovereign.

We can glance quickly at the case of the Ottoman Empire. The sultan had his own military forces early: the "servants of the Porte," or *kapikulu*, composed of janissaries—about 50,000 men in the seventeenth century—and six companies of mounted bodyguards, and the frontier service or *seratkulu*, probably about 100,000 men. The system also included *sipahi*, or knights provided for life with estates, who served from March to October in wartime. The *sipahi* concerned themselves more often with managing their land than with military duty, and in the seventeenth century they became a kind of back-up force without real military value. In addition, the *sekban*, troops under the orders of the provincial governors, appeared fairly early; they were supported by taxes levied by the governors and were paid only in wartime. The *sekban* represented local independent forces, sometimes rising against the sultan.

In the Hapsburg parts of Hungary, as well as in the areas conquered by the Turks, the traditional army—made up of the *banderia* belonging to the great lay and ecclesiastical nobles with immense estates or to the *comitats* (administrative districts) or towns—presented an unusual mixture of nobles and peasants. The latter (*milicia portalis*) were contributed by the nobles according to the number of *terres de serfs*, or *portae*, they owned. In the seventeenth century, for example, ten *portae* equipped three knights and three foot soldiers. This force was under the orders of the chief minister or commissioner general of the realm. The same system was used by the king for his own troops and by the rebellious Transylvanian princes. But as the nobility began to give up the military profession to attend to their estates, it became necessary to employ mercenaries, cavalry (hussars) or infantry (*hajduks*), some of whom were paid in land.

The army of the kingdom of Hungary became steadily less important among the troops fighting in that country, while the Imperial army wielded an ever-increasing power. Toward the end of the seventeenth century the national army disappeared as an independent force. The reoganization of 1715 following the Pragmatic Sanction of Charles VI preserved the "rising" of the nation in times of danger but left to the Aulic Council of War at Vienna (the *Hofkriegsrat*) the decision of when to call for it, although the costs were borne by the kingdom of Hungary. This "rising" was to include the nobility, the militias of Transylvania, Banat, and the Serbian territories, and the *milicia portalis* of the peasants. Such a levy was extremely rare in the eighteenth century, but it provided 60,000 men in 1741.

"In Poland the legal monopoly of the State did not exist in the military domain," according to A. Sawczynski. Besides the crown troops there were special troops and Cossack troops. The special troops were of various sorts: those formed by the district soldiers in the palatinates, now transformed into simple police forces; *starostes*, who in wartime formed the garrisons for the castles and royal houses; town militias; and private troops of magnates and monasteries. The armed forces of the State included the feudal nobility (*pospolite*), of whom the most important led their own bands, and also contingents from the towns. Sometimes called up, too, was the *infanterie de choix*, the peasant militia to which was assigned one-twentieth (*vingtième champ*) of the royal wealth, or the *champ du choix*; to belong to this, the peasant served six months out of a year in the company of his principality and was freed from bondage as a serf and from other obligations. These Polish militias saw frequent service. Poland became, according to General Kukiel, the classic country of insurrections, where improvised armed forces emerged from a conquered countryside to oppose foreign armies. They distinguished themselves particularly in 1655. But in the second half of the seventeenth century, military obligation became in reality more often a tax for the army.

The organization of the Polish-born Cossacks was a separate matter. The term "Cossack" actually applies to different military organizations. The *troupes de la Zaporoze* were composed of Cossacks officially registered in groups (*Pulk*), who formed the regular militia of the free Cossack population. In addition, some Cossacks were among the *starostes*, and the Cossacks of the lower Dnieper, or *Cosaques de la Sicz* (or *Setch*), not subject to the Polish government, formed independent military republics.

Examples of military obligation appear from time to time in Russian history as well, for example, at the time of the 1611 insurrection of Minine and Prince Pojarsky, who drove the Poles from Moscow. Tsar Ivan III had formed an army by tying military service to ownership of land: in the second half of the fifteenth century, estates, or *pomestié*, were awarded to fighting men for the duration of their service. Ivan IV developed the system further. In the code (*subednik*) of 1550 he divided categories of service into three degrees, or *tchines*. The highest *tchine*, composed of the aristocrats of the court, supplied the officers; the middle *tchine* consisted of 25,000 knights provided with *pomestié*; and the lowest *tchine* included poor men, who received an annual salary and served as musketeers (from 1550), cannoneers, and guards. The controlling section of the system was the cavalry of the middle *tchine*, which was assembled, half at a time, in spring and midsummer.

The system degenerated when in 1649 the men of the middle degree gained hereditary ownership of their estates. They formed a closed social group whose military interests steadily decreased; they were concerned above all to defend their privileges against the peasants now transformed into their serfs. The musketeers (*streltsy*) also became a kind of privileged unit, more interested in maintaining order than in conducting war. The spread of fire-arms in Russia in the first half of the seventeenth century called for military reforms, and in 1647 a few regiments were created for the tsar, recruited on the basis of households. The knights of the middle *tchine* were supposed to serve in them, but they tried to do away with this obligation, and in 1680 the tsar Féodor suppressed the cavalry of the middle *tchine*. Thus in eighteenth-century Russia there was no longer a militia based on the military obligation of all subjects.

In all of eastern Europe—in Russia even more than in Poland, except for the Cossacks—military service tended to be limited to a small number of privileged aristocrats.

3

Permanent Paid Armies and Military Service

THE FEUDAL obligation of forty days of service was only suitable for small-scale disputes between barons. It was inadequate for the sovereigns, who had to endow in some way those vassals kept in service longer than that term. Payment first took the form of land grants (the *fiefs de soudée* in the Holy Land), then of money. Such early forms are to be seen in Sicily, under the emperor Frederick II, in England during the Scottish and French wars, and in France around 1300. Payment became the rule in the permanent armies, in which all members—officers and men, whether fulfilling military obligations or serving as mercenaries—received some wage. Increasing the number of effectives was not easy: it meant finding them and then buying their services. Rulers were forced either to turn to contractors or to insist upon the military obligations of their subjects. The second solution came to be preferred, and after several attempts to create an effective military organization for smaller numbers of men, it led in the eighteenth century to the idea of general conscription.

MERCENARY TROOPS

Three means of obtaining soldiers were used in the course of the sixteenth century: recruitment of volunteers, who except in times of famine were given the best terms (*douceur, Handgeld*, and later *argent du roi*); impressment; and finally recourse to professional war contractors (*entrepeneurs de guerre*). This expression, used by Redlich, is anachronistic, but it expresses fairly accurately certain aspects of the actual situation. This last very convenient solution was to be found everywhere in the fourteenth century, often related to the progress toward a money economy. It reached a peak in Italy in the fifteenth century; and it led in the end to a clear separation between the roles of the military leader-contractor on the one hand, and the sovereign, the *seigneur de la guerre*, on the other.

Rulers began by turning to mercenary knights (who, in turn, recruited their own *lance*—a group of three to five armed followers) or to small bands of foot soldiers led by a *Rottmeister*. This practice gave rise to the formation of large companies composed of men from all backgrounds who, out of work because of a return of peace or temporarily lacking employment with a contractor, were looking for wars in which to fight. When these men were formed into some kind of order, ethnic groups evolved, with special forms of armament and methods of fighting, such as the *Lansquenets* of Germanic origin, the Gascons, Estradiots, even Scots, Albanians, and later Hussars from Hungary. The ruler advanced the sum necessary for recruitment before the bands were formed, and then furnished the money for their support in the form of a wage. This system was brought to its greatest refinement in Italy, with the *condotta*: the *condottiere* undertook to recruit his captains, who then signed up their own men. The *condottieri*, to whom the Italian cities entrusted their defense, very quickly sensed their power and either, like Colleone, schemed to become independent of their principalities or, like Sforza, attempted to take the places of their employers. Foreign interventions in Italy kept their ambitions in check, and their powers were eventually reduced.

Germany was to take over from Italy as the most popular area for the war contractors. As in Italy, there was no monarchical power strong enough to control their growth. They were called upon to recruit foot soldiers first in Germany, then in Switzerland and central Europe. In Switzerland the cantons managed to intervene and to become troop-suppliers themselves, thereby keeping some of the profits from the activity. Elsewhere military leaders, acting themselves as general agents, contracted with rulers to recruit an army, or with officers to recruit regiments or companies. The contract with the warlord included the *Kapitulation*, which spelled out the conditions of the agreement, and a patent issued by the sovereign. These were often accompanied by authorizations concerning the areas in which recruiting was to be done. The leader received an advance sum (*Wartegeld*) that officially engaged him and enabled him to arrange for his recruiting campaign. Also common were contracts with general agents already set up in business for themselves, in possession of an army (sometimes raised for another warlord), and hiring their services to the highest bidder.

It often happened that a ruler was unable to furnish a big enough *Wartegeld* and that the organizer advanced him the sum through bankers like Witte, Wallenstein's financial agent in Germany, or Burlamachi in England. The warlord had to mortgage lands or revenues in return for this, grant titles and estates (usually confiscated from rebels or traitors), or authorize the *Kontribution*, that is, the right of the armies to live on the countryside where they were stationed and to levy local taxes for this purpose. The military leader responsible for the maintenance of his troops became himself a businessman, employing all sorts of administrative agents.

These war contractors were of varying degrees of importance: generals who led their own armies, proprietary colonels of regiments, or proprietary captains of companies. In effect, regiments and companies had become actual property that could be accumulated, inherited, bought, and sold. The loyalty of their leaders depended on the fact that if they changed sides they lost the money owed them by the warlord. Wallenstein was the type-figure for these contractor-generals, military chiefs who were creditors of their rulers and who achieved a dangerous independence. The kings of France, Spain, England, and Sweden, as well as the States General of the United Provinces, managed to limit war contracting to regiments and companies, retaining closer control over their generals (except in the case of a foreign general leading his own army, like Bernard de Saxe-Weimar, who agreed to serve France in 1635). Similarly in the small states after 1650 the ruler, who had control over his own army, turned war into an industry, hiring out to others, like Bernard de Galen, who was Bishop of Münster, or Duke Charles IV of Lorraine (both died in 1674); or like Frederick of Brunswick-Luneburg (died in 1679) and Frederick I of Prussia, who hired out regiments to the Emperor. In the eighteenth century the kings of England resorted to this "commerce" in troops (*Soldatenhandel*) up to the time of the American Revolution.

Soldiers were hired by the captain, or for him by an agent. They were bound to him by a contract, oral if not written, and by the payment of a certain sum. Evidently the arrangements included money advanced so the recruit could get to the place of assembly, with the rest paid on his arrival; or, following the so-called Dutch system, the recruiter himself paid for the recruit's lodgings during the trip so as to keep an eye on him. To this sum was added an enlistment bonus graded according to the apparent strength of the soldier, to the degree of his military capability, and to the state of the "market" at the time. The recruit had to swear allegiance to the *articles de guerre*, which defined his duties and served as a disciplinary code. He received a fee that was variable: in Wallenstein's army in 1629 a foot soldier received one and a quarter thalers a week and a horseman, two thalers. This was for provisions, as equipment was furnished by the colonels and captains. Wages were not paid regularly, and there were occasional strikes, even actual mutinies. This happened in the Spanish army in the Netherlands between 1572 and 1607, no less than twenty-one times between 1596 and 1607. Mutinies were followed by desertion, and rivalry among enemy armies during the Thirty Years War led to the practice of luring enemy soldiers away with special bonuses and higher wages. It was at this time that the greatest number of "denationalized" mercenaries were to be found.

Recruiting was not always so difficult as one might think. Many men who drifted into the army stayed there, either because they discovered a taste for the military life or because they were trapped by debts. In Germany recruiting was widespread among peasants who were financially ruined, like Simplicissimus, Grimmelshausen's hero. Even if wages were not always paid on schedule, warfare meant some profit, and the soldiers were apt to desert and go home after fruitful pillaging. On the other hand, in the most prosperous countries like the United Provinces and England, recruiting often took place among the dregs of urban society. The return of peace was generally greeted with misgiving by officers and men, as it meant the "re-forming" of the regiments and companies—that is, their demobilization. Back pay might never be collected in these cases, and fear of this sometimes caused mutinies; it partly explains the attitude of British parliamentary forces in 1647 when attempts were made to discharge them. But in the seventeenth century, wars were frequent enough that discharged soldiers had many opportunities to reenlist in another theater of operations.

The recruiting system in the sixteenth century, and even in the seventeenth, permitted some remarkable social climbing, for example by Werth and Derfflinger, simple soldiers who became titled generals. But in the seventeenth century such promotions became less common, as it became necessary to be able to buy at least a company, except when carrying out the duties of lieutenant colonels and lieutenants—non-venal positions that opened another route for higher ambitions. Moreover, at this time, as control by the State became more firmly established, managing a company as a business (*Kompaniewirtschaft*) became less attractive and less profitable.

UTILIZATION OF MILITARY OBLIGATION IN RECRUITING REGULAR ARMIES

Although not all nobles were military men and not all commoners "civilians," it must be remembered that the military obligations of these two social orders were different. Military duty for noblemen was in principle individual; for others it was usually collective. The nobility provided most of the officers, although nobles did serve among the troops as well, as volunteers or with formal enlistment. They were found especially among the heavy cavalry (ordnance companies and ordnance security forces in France). What caused the greatest problems were the considerable variations in the number of effectives theoretically available: in France, about 10,000 in peacetime up to the time of Henry IV, five or six times that number in wartime under Francis I, and—at least officially—fifteen times as many in the 1636 levy. In times of war, appeals to the nobility were not enough, and the masses formed an overwhelming proportion of the increase in manpower. It was a general rule that wartime armies were more "plebeian" than peacetime armies. Troop reorganization, after the war was over, often took the form of a return to a generally aristocratic emphasis, for example, in France in 1447 and 1598. It was difficult to enlist, in wartime, the men who were otherwise excluded by the social order from military careers. We can divide the methods used in the different states into three categories: calling upon followers in the feudal manner, levies, and finally the first attempts at a kind of modern military service.

In the feudal monarchies, the sovereign turned to his vassals, requiring them to assemble, with their own vassals following them. The royal army was, thus, a juxtaposition of these feudal contingents. Until the eighteenth century this was a characteristic of those states in which the ruler had not succeeded in eliminating the political role of the nobility, for example, in the Empire, Poland, and Hungary.

Thus there was an Imperial army united for action in cases of attack by a common enemy, Turkish or French. This army was based on an organization of "Circles" worked out by the emperor Maximilian in 1500. The ten Circles of Empire lasted until 1805. Every "immediate" member of the Empire, that is, every direct vassal of the emperor—town or ecclesiastical or lay principality—had to furnish a contingent of soldiers in proportion to its importance. The Diet of Worms in 1521 fixed a *simplum*, or first level of mobilization, that was very low: a total of 4,000 mounted men and 20,000 foot soldiers. For this Bohemia owed 400 mounted men and 600 foot soldiers; Austria, 120 and 600; Bavaria or Württemberg, 60 and 277; the smallest contingents were four men. Whenever the total number was not reached, or when more men were needed, the next levels were put into effect, the *duplum* or the *triplum*. Wages were assured by special taxes called *mois romains*: the number of *mois romains* per year was fixed according to the number of fighting men and the duration of the mobilization. By Imperial order in 1681 the Circles were to furnish 32,000 mounted men and 76,000 foot soldiers for the *triplum*. But the German princes devoted much more attention to their own permanent armies than to the contingents they owed to the Empire, and they avoided reducing the former to supply the latter. An attempt to reorganize the Imperial army within the five western Circles was made by the Margrave Louis-Guillaume de Bade during the War of the League of Augsburg [1688–1697]; but nothing was left of his efforts after 1697. The last Imperial army was raised against France in 1793–1795; the regiment of the Elector of Mayence marched toward the frontier, while the regimental garrisons were manned by town militias.

The Polish army in wartime was also a juxtaposition of contingents led by noblemen, or magnates, and a similar arrangement existed in Hungary up to the end of the seventeenth century. In these two countries mobilization was subject to the will of the Diet, but as was pointed out above, that organization was vulnerable to rebellions and civil wars. In the early seventeenth century the Evangelical League and the Holy League in Germany, and in Poland the armed confederations, were able to use units of these armies for their own ends. We should add that during the Wars of Religion in France it was suggested by the Protestants that the royal army should consist of a union of Catholic and Protestant armies. But the usefulness of this kind of composite force was much reduced in the eighteenth century, and the part played by the army of the Circles in the disaster of Rossbach is well known.

The levies ordered by the sovereign required all men to take part in the king's armies, and assigned responsibility for arrangements and costs to the provinces, towns, and trade guilds. Under this system, employed only in times of distress, the government characteristically concerned itself little with how the troops were raised. The system was often based on force. In some cases impressment was resorted to: recruiters hired by those responsible for the levy simply carried men away bodily. As late as 1704, French recruiters were authorized to resort to impressment. Sometimes such extremes were not necessary, and the towns and guilds found men to hire—former soldiers, adventurous youths, men out of work, or prisoners who were set free to serve the king. Often municipal authorities profited by the levy in getting rid of undesirable elements. The sovereign invited such action; up to the middle of the seventeenth century he often ordered former soldiers, beggars, and tramps to sign up without delay. England made use of this system to levy troops for service in Scotland or on the continent.

After the great levy of 1636, the use of force in recruiting was again seen in France when an army of 200,000 was raised during the war with Holland. The abuses at this time led to the formation of an organized military service, the royal militia, to augment the number of fighting men during wartime.

This was not the first step in this direction. We must look back still further to find its origins, probably to England in the fourteenth century, with the organizing of archers, then to Switzerland, finally to France under Charles VII, in the middle of the fifteenth century. In 1445 and during the last years of the Hundred Years War, France possessed a permanent army in which the ordnance companies, which were mounted troops, were the essential element. To acquire an infantry it was necessary to appeal to the common people. In 1448 the *francs-archers* were created: each parish was to furnish one bowman, who would be exempted from taxes and who had to undergo training every Sunday. Louis XI tried to create a corps of 16,000 of these men, divided into archers, crossbowmen, and pikemen, under four commanders. The result was disappointing, and he discontinued the effort in 1480. Francis I took up the idea with provincial legions (1534): Seven provinces were to serve as bases for recruiting for legions with permanent structures, which would be named after the provinces. This project, too, had to be abandoned. Although they were different in method, the *francs-archers* and provincial legions stemmed from the same attitude, then prevalent, that the military obligation of the peasants was not individual but collective in nature. In the former case, the parish owed a bowman; in the latter, the province owed a legion. The king interfered seldom or not at all in the choice of the men to be delivered.

The provincial legions were inspired by the Spanish example: the king of Spain had imposed on his provinces the task of raising and supporting the *tercios*, for which a structure was perfected between 1534 and 1536, with some adjustments to be made in 1562. With its regimental organization (ten companies of 250 men, with commissary, medical, police, and chaplain services), the *tercio* was the most successful form of permanent troops in the sixteenth century. But recruitment by provinces was eventually almost completely abandoned, although several attempts to revive it—especially in 1635—were made. If the money was raised, it was often diverted from its destination, and the troops received nothing. There were several later examples of this kind of provincial force in France, but they were short-lived organizations under the regional administration of the State, like the *Septimanie* dragoons regiment (1745), which was more like a special local militia. Regional recruiting was reduced to assigning the provinces to certain units as recruiting areas, and the names of the provinces were then often given to the regiments. After the sixteenth century, recruiting for permanent armies became much less restricted. Recruiters "found" men wherever the troops went, and the provincial names of the regiments no longer meant very much.

Nevertheless, because of the difficulty in finding enough men, attempts were made in the eighteenth century to bring back some form of regional recruiting. The Hapsburgs assigned a province or half a province to "national regiments" of the Austrian Netherlands. Local authorities were asked to assist the recruiters (*Placard de Bruxelles*, 1758). In France, the formation of regiments from recruits was attempted in 1760: each had its own recruiting zone, or its "market" for men (Paris, Rouen, and so forth). The effort had to be given up; there was a complete breakdown of the association of obligation with military service.

Instituting these forms of military service led to the creation of a society of professionals bound to a term of military service which was limited at first to the duration of the war, then to an undetermined period. Not until Louvois was the length of engagement fixed at three, then at six, years; and in fact it was then usually renewed. Distinction was no longer made between men who had voluntarily joined the army, those who had been impressed, and those sent by their communities. All signed formal engagement papers (except the "volunteers," to be discussed later). Many remained willingly or stayed because they were unable to find another means of living.

THE TREND TOWARD
CONSCRIPTION

Consolidation of the power of the State meant primarily a reduction of the authority of intermediate bodies—provinces, towns, guilds—who found their roles reduced to those of agents. Consequently we observe a reappearance of the idea of military service as an individual obligation, no longer a collective responsibility. All citizens in western Europe were registered when they reached adulthood (from sixteen to twenty years of age, according to the various countries or periods of history; in Prussia registration took place at ten). Men thus became soldiers not now because of a formal enlistment but in virtue of a listing and appointment in which they had no part. Such practices arose from the growing need for soldiers and the increasing reluctance to serve. In effect, allowing the towns themselves to collect the men required by the king meant that they were competing with the regimental recruiters. On the other hand, since there was no question of taking everyone, it was necessary to choose among the candidates, eliminating those who were too old, who had families, who were too young or weak, who were indispensable to the economy, or whose departure would lead to a social decline for their families. There was a considerable number left over. In Sweden and Prussia, countries with small populations, a large proportion of the adult men became soldiers. In parts of France with relatively low population density, the method was to draw lots among the *"miliciables."* This kind of conscription did not mean universal military service. It should be noted, by the way, that the word "conscription" came into general use at the end of the eighteenth century to designate a military structure freed from the framework of collective obligation and exemptions then judged to be abused; it was a method under which men were put directly into the regular troops.

Sweden was the first country to organize a permanent army based on the principle of military obligation, and this was only achieved after an evolution that lasted nearly a century and a half. In 1544 the *Riksdag*, using the lists of all who had served in the most recent conflict, instituted an annual census of men and claimed the right to call up one out of five or six whenever it should be necessary. In each parish equal numbers of men were formed into groups, and committees chose one militiaman from each group, according to physical, family, and social criteria that became more and more complex. This system was the basis for the formation by Gustavus Adolphus of a Swedish army with a national character. In 1617–1618 Sweden was divided into eight major military regions for the purpose of recruiting at first one, then several, regiments. The plan excepted certain towns, the property of the highest aristocracy, and mining districts. It produced a force of about 40,000 men, some 4 percent of the population. Gustavus Adolphus dipped into this militia to form his army.

The system was not imposed without protest, for peasants were sometimes taken from their farms without adequate consideration of individual circumstances. In 1644 the groups of men from which the militiamen were chosen were replaced with groups of farms, or *rotar* (singular: *rote*), which had to pay the costs of one soldier. A military survey and assessment was worked out. The loss of crown lands, from which the Swedish army drew the greatest part of its men, and military reverses—among them the defeat of Fehrbellin by the elector of Brandenburg in 1675 and events of the War of Scania (1675-1679)—required a general restructuring of this method of recruiting.

The new system was the *Indelningsverket*, instituted by Charles XI in 1682 along with other general reforms. Some of the lands that had been granted to the nobility were repossessed by the crown, and certain properties were designated for the support of government officials or military men. Except for the royal guard and the artillery, the entire army was based on the *Indelningsverket* (the verb *indela* has two meanings: to divide into groups and to allot). For the infantry, all the landholders of the *rotar* had to give to the *indelt* (plural: *indelta*), who was a kind of militiaman, an allotment of cultivable land and grazing land, and build him a wooden house of a standard model. This meant that he only needed to be given 100 thalers in cash each year. When the soldier was at war, his neighbors (**Knektehallare**) were to cultivate his land for the support of his family. Similar arrangements were made for supporting cavalrymen and officers. The lands allotted to the colonel were in the center of the province, those of the captain were in the center of a group of *rotar* corresponding to a company, and similarly for lower grades. Military villages were formed by the small units, which were connected by a remarkable system of roads leading to the ports of embarkation. The arrangement was worked out for defensive purposes, but it allowed Charles XII to have an army well enough trained to fight away from home in central and eastern Europe. The *Indelningsverket*, greatly modified, was to last until 1901. It freed the State for a long time from the burden of providing subsistence for the men, although we should note that after Poltava Charles XII had to resort to a kind of conscription in order to rebuild his armed forces.

In the West, several states—Spain and England among them —had by the end of the seventeenth century passed beyond the stage of local militias and had organized local forces on a national scale, although still intended for local service and in principle distinct from the regular army. At the beginning of the reign of Louis XIV, France had not yet reached this point. The royal militia of 25,000 men organized by Louvois continued to be an auxiliary force for the army, intended to replace the regiments in the fortresses when they went off on campaign. Suppressed in 1697, the militia was re-established at the outbreak of the War of the Spanish Succession. A new approach now meant that this auxiliary army became a reserve for the regular army. It was probably in Piedmont that this solution first appeared. From 1690 on, Piedmontese militiamen were moved into the regular troops in order to fill out ranks. In France the idea arose in 1704 to designate militia battalions as second battalions for the regiments that had only one. Introducing militiamen into the regiments was called "incorporation"; it was an early form of the kind of mixing that was to take place in the later revolutions, except that the militiamen were not volunteers. This step was very quickly by-passed during the War of the Spanish Succession, in the need to ensure recruitment for the regular troops: in 1706 men drawn by lot were sent directly into the regiments without first entering militia battalions. This was in effect compulsory army service based on lot-drawing, and the new practice proved to be very unpopular—largely because exemptions were still allowed and the practice was often abused. Desertions were frequent, except during the famine of 1709. Nevertheless, the militia allowed France to align 350,000 men against Europe.

Suppressed in 1714, the royal militia was reorganized in 1719 and again in 1726. It did not resume the character of a compulsory active service that it had held from 1706 to 1712, but it was a reserve for army recruiting during wartime. Of the 260,000 men raised for the War of the Austrian Succession, 80,000 (about 30 percent) were militiamen who had been incorporated into the army. Recruiting and maintaining the militia fell to the provincial intendants, and each *généralité* the old regional subdivisions had to furnish a fixed number of battalions. With the institution of detached companies whose men were drawn by lot, military service by the frontier populations became organized along the lines of that of the interior. Held in low esteem by the officers, the militia was so strongly disliked by civilians that the term itself was abandoned in 1771, to be replaced by the phrase "provincial troops"; there was, however, no resultant gain in prestige.

Someone has written that in the eighteenth century "Europe buried itself under militias." It was actually a second wave of forces that was created, distinct from the traditional militias; the new units were often based on the French model and were organized in a more uniform manner so that they could serve as reserves for the regular armies. In Spain it was a matter of reconstituting the militia created by Philip II. In 1704, sixteen line regiments were taken from it to replace the old regiments on the coasts. Selection by lot was introduced in Galicia in 1708, and one out of every ten men was mobilized. Finally in 1734 a reorganization took place and thirty-three regiments with 700 positions were constituted. The German princes tried to modernize their *Landmiliz*: Bavaria underwent a general levy after the defeat of Hoechstaedt in 1704; the *Landfahnen* were reorganized in 1732, and were used as sources for filling out line regiments in 1734; Saxony had to adapt its militias in 1702 and 1711.

Piedmont, where the army played a strong role at the desire of the rulers, presents an interesting case. In 1701 a general edict calling up the militia—actually a census of all eligible men—led to desertion and flight. Although during the War of the Spanish Succession the levy was reduced to 6 percent of those able to bear arms, the provincial regiments nevertheless reached a total of 30,000 men. In 1714 Field Marshal Rhebinder organized this force in a remarkable way. Ten battalions of a thousand men were formed (seven for Piedmont, two for Savoy, and one for the county of Nice), for which the levy was left to the communities.

An edict in 1737 specified the methods of recruitment: the men were to be from eighteen to forty years of age; sons of large families were to be taken by preference. Exemptions were, in principle, rare, and substitution was only allowed if the replacement were a relative bearing the same patronymic. The militiamen were assembled every year in March for six, later fifteen, days. This new force, as in France, was put under the orders of the provincial governors. At the same time, the "general militia," a combination of all the older militia units, was given a consistent military organization (illustrated, for example, by the town "battalion," later "regiment," of the citizen militia of Turin, 1734). And we must mention the levy of the *bande* in Tuscany up to 1742.

In Denmark, nine provincial regiments were raised in 1676, but they were actually composed—like the line army—of voluntary enlistees and foreigners. In 1701 the old militia, or *vaern*, was revived with a quota of peasants raised in each province. Well organized and led, the men had to serve in the defense of the country for six years. In 1719 they were put into the regular regiments, but the militia lasted through the war; and in 1733, in order to put an end to the practices of deserting and evading registration, all peasants from fourteen to thirty-six years of age were forbidden to leave their districts.

The French royal militia influenced the English militia as well. The alert of 1745–1746, when the troops of the Stuart Pretender had arrived within 150 kilometers of London, woke England from her repose and raised again the question of reorganizing the militia. This led to lively controversy, since opposition to military service was strong. The idea of militia forces was defended by Townshend, and the Seven Years War hastened the solution. The act of 1757 was the result of a compromise: the militia was reestablished, but only the City of London, the Cinque Ports, and a few other towns kept their autonomy. Drawing of lots was introduced, and the "New Militia," although unpopular, became permanent from 1769 on. Regiments of fusiliers were drawn from it for service outside the county, and in times of war it was used as a supplementary source to increase the number of effectives. This system reached a peak of usefulness between 1775 and 1802.

In Russia and Prussia different paths were followed. The Russian regular army grew out of the edicts of 1699 that followed the dissolution of the *streltsi*. The government continued to regard military service as a territorial or communal obligation. After 1647 groups of households (after the census of 1721 it was groups of individuals) had to furnish one recruit. Registration was carried out by the provinces after the 1720s, with each district responsible for one regiment. The Senate determined the frequency and size of the levies: in 1726 it was one man for every 250 inhabitants; in 1747, one for every 121. At the beginning of the century the government intervened little in the choice of recruits. All families were called upon in turn, starting with those who had the most workingmen. Then the task of selection passed into the hands of landholders and noblemen, and at the end of the century to the governors. Recruits, serving for life, had to be healthy and strong, at least fifteen years old, and over four feet nine inches tall. From 1716 on, the officers were responsible for collecting the recruits for training in garrisons under the responsibility of the governors.

The *Institution générale sur l'appel des recrues*, issued in 1766, spelled out the approved methods of recruitment. Some exemptions were allowed: *seigneurs* and leading businessmen were authorized to buy off their workers; the clergy could arrange for substitutes. About one-sixth of the population remained outside the range of the levy. The codification also specified that each recruit was to have fifty kopecks and provisions furnished by the *seigneur*. Recruits had to have their heads shaved, to prevent desertion.

At first, recruiting affected only the Russian peoples. Even when it was extended to the Mordvinians, Cheremis, and Tatars in 1722, it still continued to be a heavy burden for the Russians, and Potemkin introduced it in White Russia and the Ukraine. In the latter country a system of lot-drawing, to select one man out of 500, was set up. Potemkin hoped to limit service to fifteen years, but that could be done only in the Ukraine. Over 3 percent of the male population received regular military training, a high number compared with the western countries.

In the Brandenburg-Prussian states, the old militias were transformed in 1693 by a ruling that determined the number of men to be raised in each province. In 1703 all unmarried men were in principle required to serve in the militia. Frederick William, however, preferred to make exclusive use of the regular forces.

The *Kantonsystem* instituted in Prussia in 1733 arose from the need to reconcile the requirements of the economy with the desire of the sovereign to possess an army that was out of proportion to the size of the population—while attempting to avoid the force and brutality often practiced by the recruiters. The origins of the system are rather curious. From the beginning of the eighteenth century the captains—as was true in general throughout Europe—recruited within their own estates or landholdings (*Rittergut*). They adopted the practice of taking all the young men into service, then granting them long leaves to cultivate their lands. With the savings acquired from not having to provide for these men, the captains bought foreign recruits. Frederick William also filled his ranks in this way. Boys had to register at the age of ten, and were enrolled upon adulthood to serve for a year and a half or two years, undergoing military training; thereafter they served for two or three months every year for the rest of their lives. Each infantry regiment had to be recruited in a canton of about 5,000 households. The cavalry cantons were based on 1,800 households and remained in existence until 1763. The officers selected the recruits from the tallest and ablest enrollees, or *Obligats*. Those who owned large, important estates, as well as their heirs, were exempt from service. Also exempt were the *Kossäte*, half-serfs living on miserable holdings, who could not survive on the living allowance of a soldier and whose low pay placed a burden on their families. Finally, colonial settlers, in return for moving to Prussia, were guaranteed that they and their descendants to the third or fourth generation would be exempt from serving. This provision was reduced to sons only at the end of the century.

This system was not imposed on the western provinces, where recruiting continued to be carried out in the traditional manner. The *Kantonsystem* gave Prussia an active army which grew from 4 percent of the adult men at the beginning of the eighteenth century to 14 percent at the end. Prussian soldiers were of two kinds, then, even in peacetime: those who enlisted, usually foreigners, and the Kantonists, whose number was fixed at two-thirds of the active forces under Frederick William I and varied at about one-half under Frederick II. The artillery, however, contained subjects of the king of Prussia only.

In Austria, where levying troops was for a long time up to the local Diets, Maria Theresa had in 1752 to give up the idea of forming a militia of 24,000. In 1781, however, Joseph II introduced a system of conscription into his hereditary states of Austria and Bohemia.

Russian and Prussian rulers paid little attention to the opinions of the peasants, although as we saw above Frederick William made no attempt to impose the canton system in his western provinces.

In England, as in France, the militia was not popular, in spite of the exemptions that were intended to avoid severe disruptions in the positions or resources of individuals. The English government permitted substitution and in 1782 authorized "clubs" that could buy substitutes. Even so, revolts within the militias took place.

The French king generally forbade substitution. He did, however, allow the militia in Paris to be filled by a voluntary system from 1744 on. At the end of the eighteenth century there were in the kingdom about 600,000 men eligible for the militia, of which 14,000 were taken every year, each serving for six years. Although the burden grew less as the population increased, the militia was still very unpopular, and there were frequent failures to report for duty. The militia weighed heavily on the rural areas especially, leading to jealousies and denunciations. The lottery system was especially mistrusted, and some young men joined the regular army directly rather than leaving the matter to chance: at least they could in that way choose their captains. Rural communities organized resistance. Eligible men would contribute money to provide an indemnity for those who drew a "bad" number; next they began to use the funds to "buy" a militiaman: to be sure of being accepted, this man did not take part in the drawing, and when pronounced absent he automatically became a member of the militia. The records of grievances at the assembly of the estates-general of 1789 firmly denounced the faults of the militia, even at a time when it was almost never activated and was moreover almost entirely made up of volunteers. Meanwhile, in the late eighteenth century, several officers—among them the Chevalier des Pommelles—risking disfavor but hoping to avenge the losses of the Seven Years War, considered ways to transform the militia into a form of conscription, or to create a reserve army. An echo of this is found in the article on "Art militaire" in the *Encyclopédie méthodique* issued in 1784–1787.

The military success of Prussia and the experience gained from several militia systems led the emperor Joseph II to institute conscription for army recruiting in 1781. The troubles of 1792–1793 and the mass uprisings were to lead to the adoption in 1798 of the Jourdan law, which established compulsory military service by conscription; similar solutions, anticipated by various formulas utilized in different countries, spread throughout Europe in the nineteenth century. With conscription, military service came closer to being military duty, and the two were finally merged into the concept of compulsory universal military service.

PART II

The State and the Army

We have already encountered some State influence, since in working toward particular forms of military service the governments strongly affected popular attitudes toward such service. It is appropriate here to examine the ways in which the armies of the modern era were first organized. The subject goes well beyond the frame of the army itself. In effect, the army was a special domain, one in which the sovereign authority first prevailed; and military administration—often imposed on civilians in emergencies and under difficult conditions—served in many ways as a proving ground for other governmental operations.

In every case the State had to overcome obstacles in order to create effective armies. First of all, there were the attempts of the nobility, not only to maintain a monopoly in the military profession, but in addition to use arms in their own behalf. The State could successfully oppose such attempts only by creating a kind of "service aristocracy." Another obstacle was the prevailing diversity. All armies require a certain degree of uniformity, which can be attained either by removing men from their original surroundings or by making uniform the social and mental frameworks of all the regions that make up the State. Under the ancien regime a large regular army could be created, by the first method, outside the ordinary social structure: the best example of this was in England. Prussia illustrates the other solution, which involved the transformation of social structures in order to ensure support for an army. Although most European countries were to follow a line somewhere between the two extremes, by the eighteenth century we can distinguish between States in which a military structure is strongly evident and States whose emphasis is "civilian," in which civilian and military elements are fairly distinct.

4

Growth of Military Administration

ROYAL ARMIES, originating in the feudal armies of central and western Europe, only became the property of the sovereign after a long process of evolution. In France a Pragmatic Sanction of 1439, reaffirmed in 1583 by an ordinance of Henry III, claimed for the king the sole right to raise troops within the kingdom: all recruiters had to be endorsed or secured by a royal commission. These legal specifications were generally flouted during civil wars, and the trend was further delayed by the arrangements of the *condotta* and other contracts with "military enterprisers." In most cases of military contracting the army belonged rather to its direct military leader than to the warlord. As long as regiments and companies were bought and sold, the colonels and captains felt that they owned them, and they managed them like estates. Enlistment bound the soldier to the king ("to serve the king"), but the personal bonds, which played such an important role in the ancien regime, were established above all with the captain. Every effort was made by the sovereigns to establish direct ties between them and their soldiers, to achieve a control that would at least partly bypass the officers, and eventually military officers became simply delegates of the king.

The problems encountered by the State were of two kinds: first, it was difficult to impose rigorous discipline on men whose behavior was often violent; self-control was seldom exercised until the middle of the seventeenth century, and these men were often among the roughest and least civilized in society. Then there were the problems of forcing the proprietary officers to manage their units honestly. The history of military administration until the eighteenth century is filled with attempts to eliminate abuses.

TROOP CONTROL AND DISCIPLINE

The assumption of control over the army by the sovereign was first seen with the institution of the troop register for the purpose of keeping exact accounts of troop strength and ensuring accurate payment of wages. This led to the importance of the review (called *"montre"* in France until the sixteenth century, "muster" in Anglo-Saxon and Germanic countries), conducted by inspectors and review commissioners or war commissioners. These reviews resulted in two kinds of reports: The inventory of troops, prepared for the entire army or for one element, included lists of units with their chief officers, later other officers, and their numbers; they gave the "true state" (*"l'état au vrai"*) of the army. Second, the company rolls, also called *montres* or muster lists or muster rolls, listed all individuals present under their patronymic or assumed names, sometimes with a first name. The first such lists date from the fourteenth century, and they remained adequate until the time when desertion and abuses by officers reached major proportions, that is, until the beginning of the seventeenth century.

Cheating by the captains took several forms. There was the well-known practice of using dummy soldiers, men hired to appear in reviews in the places of men who had never been enrolled, so the company would appear to be at full strength. The captains would keep the money intended for enrollment and maintenance for the missing numbers. The dummy soldiers were soldiers borrowed from other companies, servants of the officers, or even civilians. Another abuse was to pass off new recruits as veterans. In the Spanish army such men were called *santelmos*. The captain pocketed the difference between the high pay of the experienced soldier and the ordinary wage. These practices were followed even in the military hospitals, where manpower was sometimes fraudulently computed.

To counteract such abuses it was necessary to introduce identification procedures, and from this developed modern troop-control records, with descriptive accounts of all companies indicating, besides surnames and first names, the age, birthplace, and date of enrollment for each soldier. Such documents were widely distributed in the seventeenth century, from the Polish army to the English militia; they were even kept by town militias, for example, after 1620 in Strasbourg. Sweden was somewhat ahead in troop control, and troop registers organized by companies and regiments were perfected there about 1640. France followed suit after some delay; records appeared in 1670, but only for the French guards regiments and for invalids. They took the form of enrollment lists on which were recorded descriptions of the soldiers at the time of their arrival.

The ordinance of 2 July 1716 gave rise to some remarkable troop registers: printed lists with headings and columns in which were recorded, company by company, all the men of an infantry battalion or a cavalry regiment present at the time of a general survey; they were brought up to date at irregular intervals, when the names of recruits and notes on the progress of the soldiers were added. In general, in addition to the standard information, we find the names and professions of the parents, the soldier's profession, his description (height, skin and eye color, unusual characteristics), the length of service, re-enlistments, promotions, departure from the company by death, desertion, or leave. These troop registers are interesting documents, not just for our understanding of military society but for insight into civilian society as well. At that time few individuals were actually described anywhere. Except for travelers, who in the eighteenth century were given vaguely descriptive passports for their protection, descriptive identification was considered for some time to be an intrusion into one's privacy, something imposed on those who were for some reason under suspicion. As a price for the uniformity it was seeking, the army had to organize a system of identification. In the eyes of those who were affected the army appeared to have opened a door for civil administrators, and probably for fraudulent activities as well.

The abuses did not disappear completely, and even under the Empire in France captains were in no hurry to report desertions: they would have been taken as evidence of poor management. The return of a soldier who had left on an impulse could always be hoped for, and so the captain kept his pay while his comrades shared his rations. After a battle the deserters were added to the list of those killed, for men lost in battle were replaced at the expense of the government. Malpractices were reduced in peacetime, however, during periods of normal administration.

The problem of troop support, and particularly of wages, was linked to the elimination of abuses. In the seventeenth century, captains usually paid the men their wages in cash; with this they had to support themselves. The Spanish army in Flanders offers a good illustration of the progress in military administration in the matter of troop support. In spite of the different *asientos*, or contracts, drawn up by Charles V and Philip II, these sovereigns lacked the money to pay wages without considerable delays. Since a soldier who was not paid mutinied, or at least refused to march, an advance (*socorro*) had to be granted for living expenses. Moreover, necessary supplies could not be furnished regularly without resort to private enterprise. The captains, therefore, dealt with contractors for bread, clothing, weapons, and medical supplies. Philip II introduced the authority of the

State into this trade, and the government took over the furnishing of supplies with the institution of the *proveedores de viveres* (suppliers) and supply stores. The same arrangements held for clothing after 1594. To obtain the necessary bread and munitions, the *proveedores* turned to private contractors and arms dealers. Horses were supplied on credit, their cost deducted from wages (1590). This arrangement had to be extended in most of the armies to food, and it often spread as well to other supplies—clothes, for example—with the institution of the *masse*, or the common coffer into which money necessary for repairs was placed. The *masse* evidently appeared toward the end of the seventeenth century.

Wages, reduced by deductions made for supplies, continued to be paid irregularly, especially during foreign operations in which they were delayed by problems of currency exchange. And in 1638 we find French soldiers, fearing that they would not receive their wages beyond the Rhine border, demanding an advance before they would cross the river. In the Germanic countries during the Thirty Years War, the *Kontribution* assigned to the civilian population the responsibility for paying the wages (according to the Halberstadt ordinance issued by Wallenstein in 1625). Irregular payment had a bad effect on the troops: because of the delays, officers were inclined to close their eyes to marauding, while payment of arrears led to careless spending by the soldiers. Troops were paid more regularly in France after the reorganization carried out by Michel Le Tellier and Louvois. By the end of the seventeenth century conditions were similarly improved in most armies, but the War of the Spanish Succession was to revive the difficulties.

One problem, especially in wartime, was the simultaneous payment of troops of diverse backgrounds, with various wages paid in different currencies according to the particular contracts and countries served in. As a general rule, foreign corps received higher wages than national regiments. In the army of Gustavus

Adolphus, Swedish regiments received a wage half that of the German corps. In the French army of the eighteenth century, pay for the German, Italian, and especially Swiss regiments was a little higher than that for the French units.

It became customary to pay national regiments according to units based on the wage and ration of an ordinary soldier. Non-commissioned officers were entitled to a certain number of pay units (*payes*). Accordingly, in the Netherlands, a unit of 300 men received 400 *payes* in 1552. The captain received ten, *enseignes* five each, sergeants, billeting officers, and *clercs*, two each. One and a half *payes* went to a halberdier, a drummer, and a fifer. Such a system provided a salary scale for whatever amount was to be distributed. Pay units varied, too, according to the weapons carried and the functions within the company: in the Empire around 1621, cuirassiers received sixteen to eighteen florins a month, arquebusiers eleven to sixteen and a half florins, pikemen six to nine, and musketeers seven to eight. Such variations were due to the fact that the maintenance of the weapons was more or less burdensome for the individual, and also to the unequal prestige of the different weapons and the different degrees of difficulty in enlisting men with particular skills.

Rations were handled in the same manner. The unit for food rations persisted throughout the eighteenth century in the French army, and it varied little, at least in theory. An Imperial ordinance of 1630 fixed the daily ration at two pounds of bread, one pound (later one and one-half) of meat, and two measures of beer or wine. Officers received a certain number of ration units according to rank. In the French army, after Louvois, the scale of rations for the troops was one unit for a foot soldier, one and a half for a dragoon, and two for a cavalry trooper. And of course the trading of rations could supplement wages.

We can assume that the allowances received by soldiers in the eighteenth century were generally fairly equal in value from one army to another. In France the wage was fixed at six sous a day for the infantryman until 1762, when it was raised to eight. This was roughly equal to the wages of an average tradesman or peasant, but it included Sundays and holidays, and there was no risk of losing one's job. It should be noted that the variations in wages among different corps of the same army reflected a difference in the degree of discipline. In France, foreign troops were better paid, but they were more rigorously controlled as well.

The Dutch method, according to which the recruit came immediately under the orders of the army at the moment he was signed on, spread throughout Europe in the middle seventeenth century. Nevertheless, instances can still be found in France during the eighteenth century of young men who enlisted in the autumn on the specific condition that they were not to join their corps until spring. The enlistment bonus, half of which was paid upon arrival, varied according to the physical and other aptitudes of the soldier, but a more important factor was the available supply of recruits. Bonuses, which had fallen to nothing in 1710, rose rapidly after 1727, and a maximum of 60 livres was therefore imposed. Recruiting officers actually had to give more, but at their own expense, and the real bonuses sometimes rose to several hundred livres. On the other hand, special gifts to the men after a victory, although still common during the Thirty Years War, disappeared gradually as the State assumed greater control over the officers in the administration of the army.

Conscript armies encountered similar problems, and their administrators turned for supplies partly to private enterprise but also to requisitioning. Wages were paid generally along the lines of the system outlined above, but there were no enlistment bonuses. A certain sum was turned over to each man, however, either when he left home to join the army or when he was taken into the corps. This sum, furnished by the collectives on whose behalf the soldier was serving or—in Russia—by the feudal overlord, was supposed to be used for personal equipment.

The royal militias differed little from this pattern. In England the "marching guinea" was granted to a member of the New Militia. Militiamen's pay was slightly less than that of the regular troops (it was five sous a day in France), and the weapons and clothes that were issued were usually not of the best quality. In the English New Militia they were reissued every twelve years, which was not often enough.

Within the system built up by articles of war and royal ordinances, discipline in the sixteenth and early seventeenth centuries rested primarily with the captains, shifting increasingly to the entire hierarchy of the regiment. The captain handled the misdemeanors of his men except for capital crimes, one of which was desertion. The regiment had a court of justice presided over by the colonel. In the sixteenth-century mercenary armies, fixed terms of service were seldom established, but discipline became more enforceable when a man signed up for a limited engagement—three and later six years in France after the time of Louis XIV—and when pay rations were issued more regularly. Discharges were granted theoretically at the start of the winter quarter following the expiration of the term of engagement, on the condition that the companies were not left with too few men. Time off for leaves and other absences was deducted, and the soldier could not leave if any debts to the company were unpaid. Men often served beyond their terms, therefore, and some reenlisted. Enforcement of discipline made everyone more aware of the conduct of the soldiers.

A soldier could escape the rigorous discipline only by desertion, and this became the greatest source of trouble for the armies of the eighteenth century. Over a period of twenty-seven years during the reign of Frederick William I, the Prussian army had no less than 30,000 deserters. In Saxony the infantry had 8,500 deserters for every 20,000 men between 1717 and 1728, and the cavalry had 750 out of 5,400. The French army appears to have been especially affected: one man out of four left his regiment during the War of the Spanish Succession. They were not all actually lost to the army; in fact, desertion was often fictitious, since the fraudulent practice of enlisting more than once in order to accumulate the advance payments made on the enlistment bonus naturally enlarged the number of desertions recorded. Recruiters were partly responsible for this, as some of them did not hesitate to entice men from other companies. As a consequence there existed throughout Europe a number of "*rouleurs*," moving from one regiment to another, even from one army to another; their total numbers were not high, but they may have represented about 10 percent of the enrollments in the troop records of the French army.

The campaign against desertions became more systematic with the increase and improvement of records. Deserters were generally condemned to the dungeons or to the galleys. Between 1716 and 1775 in France the death penalty was inflicted on one out of every three deserters, drawn by lot. The harsh penalty led to some secret assistance to deserters on the part of the civilian population, and the number of pardons for those who returned had to be increased. Agreements were signed by governments for prisoner exchanges, but they were not carried out very seriously, even between allied countries, because the competition by recruiters was so vigorous. By the end of the eighteenth century, troop control in France had succeeded in reducing desertion to about 4,000 cases per year, some two percent of the effectives.

Evidence that the men were coming increasingly under State authority is seen in the treatment accorded to prisoners of war. At first, only those prisoners who could offer ransom—that is, officers and gentlemen—were of interest. In the sixteenth century all others were frequently massacred. Only the fear of reprisal prevented the killing of prisoners. The captains had to buy back any of their men who had been captured, so in the late sixteenth century various procedures for exchanging prisoners grew up, based on negotiations between the colonels and captains of the opposing armies. Meanwhile the State began to intervene, and in 1599 the States General of the United Provinces negotiated an exchange with Spanish troops. Several agreements of this sort were concluded between French and Spanish governments during the war of 1635 to 1659. But intervention by governments often prolonged the captivity because of lengthy, difficult negotiations in which political considerations naturally played an important part. In the eighteenth century the idea arose of creating, once peace was achieved, "cartels" for the exchange of prisoners in future wars. Exchanges were to be made automatically, one man for another of equal rank. In the case of a surplus on one side, a ransom equal to one month's pay was to be paid. Once the States entered into these exchanges, the captains could no longer be sure of getting back their own men, as these might be put into other units.

The assumption by the State of control over the men was reflected, too, in changes in the formulas for enlistment. Thus in France the formula, "soldier of lord . . . , captain of the . . . regiment," was replaced about 1745 by, "soldier of the . . . regiment, . . . company." In general the developing military administration tended to take many functions away from the captains. Attempts were made almost simultaneously in France and Prussia to relieve them of the responsibility of recruiting: in France, regiments of recruits were created (1760–1767), and in Prussia the *Grosse* was inaugurated, an overall recruitment for the army by the king himself (1763–1786). We should note, too, the takeover of the companies by the French king in 1762 and the progressive abolition after 1776 of the sale of offices, whose value was reduced by one-quarter with each transfer.

By these processes the armies of the western countries developed along lines similar to those armies that were created as whole units by State powers, as in Prussia and Russia. The armed forces that were to oppose each other during the Wars of the French Revolution and the Napoleonic Empire were firmly under the control of the States.

MILITARY OFFICERS AND CIVIL ADMINISTRATORS

In the armies of the sixteenth and early seventeenth centuries, personal man-to-man relationships constituted the major internal ties, and the moral authority of the leader was thus of the greatest importance. We must not be surprised to find troops led by prelates like Cardinal Maurice of Savoy, Cardinal Sourdis, or the Cardinal Infante of Spain. Military leaders could not be courtiers. The most highly esteemed were old soldiers whose physical courage and bravery were proved. Such leaders, concerned primarily about the welfare of their men, were often imperfect administrators; at the very least, they would close their eyes to those offences which did not directly threaten troop discipline or performance. The sovereign, therefore, found it necessary to create a military administration without using military men.

That administration came into being gradually with the appointment of civilians to positions of control over this or that weak spot in the army. Little by little these positions were coordinated into an administrative pyramid. Two areas, however, remained in military hands. One was military justice, with its war councils or courts. A military police system was formed that was to prosecute offenders and carry out sentences, and its chief, who held a colonel's rank, was the provost (the *écoulète* in German regiments, the *barrachel* in Spain). In France a provost general of a unit was the highest authority in matters of military justice. Another area that remained under military control was the internal detailed administration of the companies, left to the quartermasters and other staff under the authority of the captains. Later, when the regiment became more important in France, the majors, aides, and so forth acquired more responsibility.

Under Charles VII the first coherent system of control over

troop supply in France was initiated. The regular war funds were used for expenses relating to ordnance companies, but maintenance for other troops, much the larger part of the army from the seventeenth century on, was paid for from special funds. It should be noted that the artillery always had a separate fund. The manner in which pay was distributed varied little, except in the armies of the *condottieri*. For example, in the Netherlands after the time of Charles V, the review inspectors carried out reviews every three months, sometimes without prior notice; the treasurers turned the pay over to the captains upon the recommendation of the inspectors, who were subject to the approval of the highest military authorities, the captain general or the governors of the provinces. The Spanish monarchy made important advances in military administration in the sixteenth century. The review inspector (*veedor*) was all-powerful. The master of accounts (*contador*) and the treasurer (*pagador*) could do nothing without his signature. He was attended by armed guards. In addition there were the supply commissioners (*proveedores*), and from Madrid the *contaduria mayor de cuentas* (accounting department) controlled all details of the entire Spanish army.

The immense war effort set in motion by Richelieu demanded the creation of a major administrative section. The commissioners of war assumed greater powers than the review inspectors, as it was their responsibility to control the quality and the sources of the recruits, and as a consequence they intervened in company affairs. The armies came under the management of commissioners, senior administrative officers whose powers were rapidly separated from those of the provincial intendants.

While the army intendants had the upper hand in the matter of keeping the forces supplied, the provincial intendants, along with the provincial governors, maintained an important role in military administration. In the eighteenth century, provincial intendants kept a watch over recruiting and heard the complaints of the civilians concerning abuses by recruiters. Occasionally they even took part in recruiting, as for the regiments of recruits of 1760. They also assisted in searching for deserters and in controlling soldiers on leave. They supervised the commissioners of war in their territorial subdivisions and held authority over the military hospitals. And, finally, they were responsible for the levy and support of the militias. The provincial intendants corresponded directly concerning all these matters with the secretary of state for war. In France a militiaman could evade the watchful eye of this senior provincial officer only when his unit left the district; within a particular region the intendant supervised everything, until registration and record-keeping were established for the battalions.

Conditions were similar in Piedmont, where all contracts between officers and munitions suppliers had to be authorized by the king. The *contador generale* of the army was both an administrator and a judge in cases between individual citizens and military personnel. Appeal was made to a supreme tribunal composed of the *contador generale*, the auditor general of the army, and a member of the Accounts Office. Thus in most countries, maintenance of the army, some disciplinary matters, and relations between civilians and military personnel fell within the jurisdiction of civil administrators.

Special secretaries for military affairs appeared fairly early in the government councils. The first secretary of state responsible for military affairs in France was Servien (1635). Following the work carried out by Le Tellier, Louvois organized the War Ministry. In the kingdom of Piedmont, the general war commissioners, together with the local commissioners, became the War Secretariat, which was enlarged and reorganized in 1717. In many countries, in line with their governmental traditions, a collective board or war council was created, an institution that was briefly copied in France under the Regency, within the framework of the *polysynodie*. In Austria the *Generalkriegskommissariat* (1650), soon backed up by the *Generalproviantamt*, which controlled troop provisioning, was the first step toward a centralized war administration. The *Hofkriegsrat* (the Aulic Council of War) became the single link between the Emperor and his generals in 1675, especially after the loss of his dependency of Graz as a military confine (1705). In 1752, with the reforms of Haugwitz under Maria Theresa, the powers of the *Hofkriegsrat* (command) and the *Generalkriegskommissariat* (pay, discipline, troop maintenance) were clearly identified.

England followed the same course, although with some confusion. A war minister was not to appear there until after the Crimean War. Even in the eighteenth century, military administration was split among the war secretary created by Charles II for cavalry and infantry, the Ordnance Board organized at the same time for armament and artillery, the Treasury, which controlled provisioning, the Paymaster, and finally the Board of General Officers created in 1706, with more strictly military responsibilities. Under William III, who himself commanded his armies, the war secretary received his orders directly from the sovereign. This was a unique situation, however, and the war secretary's office was in fact under the secretaries of state for the northern department (concerned particularly with European matters) and the southern department (directing American affairs). The secretaries of state not only transmitted the king's orders to the war secretary, who in turn kept them informed about the needs of the army, but during the Seven Years War went so far as to give orders concerning troop movements within their departments. In addition, they held power over the militia. This was the highest degree of civil power to be found anywhere. Another evidence of civil control over the army was the creation in 1703 of the office of Comptroller of the Army and Accounts, which according to a very strict royal warrant controlled all equipment and pay distributed after 1707.

The general tendency was not followed in Prussia, where the director of finance, war, and lands merged civil and military affairs, making the former subsidiary to the latter.

Gradually the secretariats or councils built up staffs directed by specialists in the essential areas such as muster-lists, pay, and troop supply. In some countries a separation of powers was established according to which the war minister was responsible for administration and the king's military cabinet ruled on operations. This was the case in Prussia, Austria, and Russia. In France and England this distinction was not formalized, despite the existence of the Board of General Officers. A true military cabinet was not constituted until the time of William III in England, and Louis XIV, with Chamlay, in France. In 1788 a War Council was formed by the generals in France, to balance the effect of Louis XVI's lack of interest in military matters.

Officers reluctantly accepted the idea of control by legislators or administrative staffs who were not military men. In France it required all the power of Louvois and his successors to tame them. Spain, Piedmont, Bavaria, and Austria underwent similar evolutions, often profiting by the French example. In contrast, in the monarchies of eastern Europe different problems were manifested, since the civil administration itself had a military character. This was true in Russia, but especially so in Prussia, where many civil posts were filled by former military officers. Nevertheless it can be stated that nearly everywhere—either because the army was the major preoccupation of the sovereigns or because the emergencies faced by military administrators required immediate solutions—military administration, far from lagging behind other administrations, in many ways led the way for them.

CIVILIAN POPULATIONS AND TROOP SUPPORT

Troops were maintained by the civilian population, either directly or indirectly. In the first case, an army took or demanded from the inhabitants what it needed. The usual practice was to buy provisions, but the purchase was often carried out by requisitioning, or forced sales with deferred payment. In the second case, the State or the local communities entered into the dealings by guaranteeing to supply provisions which they financed through tariffs or special taxes. Both methods were used by invading armies as well as by national armies.

In the presence of an enemy army the people were at the mercy of the victor. The idea of citizens' rights was established only with great difficulty, and it was probably hindered by universal military obligation. The soldiers felt that they were not bound to respect civilians who took part in acts of war, and the more they were subjected to secret attacks and ambushes, the more cruel and remorseless they became. Civil rights required a clearer distinction between combatants and noncombatants, a distinction which developed slowly after the late seventeenth century, along with the growing separation of civilian from military populations; a civilian sniper or guerrilla came to be considered an exception and was treated with great severity. Pillaging of towns became less common as civilians no longer took part in defending their towns other than in auxiliary capacities, and as the major strongholds included fortresses in which defenders took refuge. Also, surrender according to certain conventions became more common, at least in western Europe.

Occupying forces only slowly abandoned the practices of "safeguarding" and the *Kontribution*. Victorious armies living off the country ran the risk of exhausting their means of subsistence. Civilian populations tried to hide food from them, and foraging parties had to go increasing distances. For these reasons military leaders tried to conclude agreements with local authorities to guarantee the provisioning of the troops in exchange for "safeguards," or protection for the civilians. Such agreements were fairly common in the seventeenth century and were sometimes endorsed by government authorities as the power of the States grew. An example is the "contribution treaty" arranged in 1710 between the "directors of contributions" of the States Gen-

eral of the United Provinces and the representatives of the intendant of Picardy and Artois to cover those parts of the area north
of the Somme. In exchange for a payment of 800,000 livres in
coin, the inhabitants were free to move about and their property
was to be secure.

When a national army was stationed in an area, it was necessary to regulate the ways in which troops obtained provisions, for
their base stations and when on the march. A system of military
stages or halting places appeared in France in the middle of the
sixteenth century. Then, spreading outward from Savoy, a country that had been occupied by the French, it was adopted by the
Duke of Alba in the military corridors used by Spanish troops on
their way to the Netherlands. The innovation consisted of hand-
ing over to the villages—not to the armed forces—the money for
provisioning, at least for that part that was to be covered by
indirect charges to the population.

There were two kinds of stations. In France there were permanent stations established in towns on the regular routes followed
by the troops; from the reign of Henry II on, France had a network of such stations. Station inspectors supervised the *étapiers*
or entrepreneurs who undertook to supply the troops. In addition, there were temporary stations organized by the officers of
an army as it approached an area; upon approval by the local
authorities, the contracting parties signed statements of terms.
Transport was arranged for by the *étapiers* or by wagon-drivers
with whom the officers contracted for specified transport. Military stations spread over Europe in the seventeenth century. Put
under the authority of the general directors of forage, provisions,
and stations in 1703, the stations in France were in theory two
leagues apart, giving some flexibility in the movement of troops
and allowing the armies to be scattered among the civilian populations.

As the urban fortresses were outgrown or fell into disrepair, the
lodging of men-of-war was charged to the citizens, although the

nobility and certain privileged individuals were exempted, at least
in France. Payment was made in kind or in cash, and to the
charges was added a provision for the *ustensile*: a soldier lodged
in the house of a citizen was to have a fire, a candle, cooking
utensils, and salt. In peacetime and during winter months the
government tried to spread the troops around so that citizens
would not be overwhelmed by costs. The cavalry, especially, was
dispersed among the villages. The municipal authorities in
agreement with the officers assigned the lodgings.

The arrangement was not without difficulties. Often the town
officials undertook to lodge military men by requiring the
townsmen to pay taxes equivalent to lodging and the *ustensile*:
with this money they built barracks, particularly in England,
Flanders, and Germany. In France the preferred practice was to
buy old houses and keep them up in rudimentary fashion to
house men and horses. In cases of large bodies of men, however,
recourse was had to rooms in the citizens' houses. Plans made in
1720 for billeting troops envisaged the existence of lodging houses
in all the halting places.

Housing soldiers with townsmen mixed together armies and
civilian populations. Streets and squares took on a military aspect, and the lives of the inhabitants were given a new rhythm by
military trumpet calls, exercises, and reviews. Gradually, at a
pace that varied from country to country as the practice was
encouraged or imposed by the State, the towns built barracks
with the lodging funds. This led to a concentration of troops in
towns. The tendency to transform contributions to the army into
taxes, which was evident in France, reached its greatest extent in
Prussia with the institution of the *Kriegskontribution*, the military
tax which supplied the war treasury. The repair and supply of
forts, however, were not usually included in such arrangements.

The provinces and the town authorities tried to avoid billeting
troops and besieged the king with petitions. Intendants often
undertook to defend them, though we should note that, if a

degree of discipline was guaranteed, some administrators, like Turgot in Metz in 1698, recognized that the presence of troops was a source of business for a poor country because of purchases by the troops and money spent by the officers. By contrast, militias meant maintenance costs as well as the burden of actual service, a fact that did not increase their popularity, at least in France and England.

Relationships between troops and civilians were not without conflicts and clashes. In theory it was up to the civil authorities to prevent them and to the civil courts to deal with them. But for a long time military personnel played an important part in regulating such matters. This was naturally true in Prussia, where precedence of the military over the civil authority had become a State maxim. There, superior officers investigated cases of shortages or fraud resulting from acts of the civil functionaries. They regulated the costs of provisions in the garrison towns. Conflicts in which civilians and military men were opposed were judged by mixed tribunals always presided over by military officers. And it was always a general who chaired the provincial council, the highest regional authority.

It was different in France, but military jurisdiction did not always stop exactly at the boundaries of the regiment. On the one hand, the governor, who was responsible for public order, was a military officer; and the mounted constabulary, which was created in the sixteenth century and reorganized in 1720 and charged with policing the highways and the countryside, was a military body. The constabulary's tribunals judged glaring minor offenses of military men, and it was also involved in looking after individual members of the armed forces, particularly those on leave. On the other hand, we have already seen that civil administrators, the intendants, intervened to a great extent in military administration. The intendant naturally played an important part in all matters concerning relationships between civilians and soldiers. Matters of billeting and the halting stations were in his jurisdiction. When his subordinates, to whom the citizens carried their complaints, informed him of abuses by men of the armed forces, the intendant would inform the minister of war. Such complaints increased in the eighteenth century, partly because of the increase in the number of effectives, but also because the civilians felt that the intendants were giving them better protection and because they were increasingly rejecting military involvement. The number of complaints was not reduced until progress was made toward housing troops in military barracks.

Thus the State was imposing order throughout Europe, whether by subordinating civilians to military authorities or by isolating the army from the populace.

THE STATE AND FORMER SOLDIERS

In the sixteenth century, State control over military men lasted only as long as they were in active service. After a campaign gentlemen went home to their estates. Soldiers had to re-enlist elsewhere, return to their homes, find another job, or beg. With the creation of permanent armies it became more difficult for men who had served for a long time to be reabsorbed into society. And the problem of maimed soldiers was added to the problem of the men who had become too old to serve. The king felt no more than a moral debt to the nobility, as war wounds or death were a part of the "blood tax" which exempted them from other charges, but for the working classes it was different. Actually, after the sixteenth century noblemen who were found in the armies were increasingly those without property, and the fate of many a crippled or aged gentleman was the same as that of former soldiers of common origin. Thus there appeared the very difficult problem of what was called in Italy "the dead army."

Signing up for life service or re-enlisting kept fairly elderly men in the service. Some particularly hardy veterans were always kept in the companies to instruct recruits and serve as examples. In spite of the soldiers' scorn for servants and for the world that swarmed around the armies, some who had nothing better to do followed the troops, hoping for small jobs. Many were unable to readjust to civilian life and took to begging; among them were the maimed and crippled, who occasionally formed dangerous bands. Thus the problem of ex-soldiers was one of both charity and public order. As such it was approached in many ways, according to the different attitudes held toward all poor men and beggars.

As charity was one of the responsibilities of the Church, monasteries were obliged to take in former soldiers as lay brothers or oblates. In Protestant countries this obligation was passed on to charitable institutions which had taken over church property. By the end of the sixteenth century this solution was no longer possible because of the growing number of ex-soldiers and the fact that their behavior was hardly compatible with monastic life as disrespect for religion increased among the troops. The monasteries preferred to pay a pension to the oblates imposed on them, to permit them to live outside the convent, and to take in only non-military lay assistants. The situation was perhaps less serious in Protestant countries, although the charitable institutions were certainly not equipped to face the influx of ex-soldiers produced during the Thirty Years War.

The rulers began to take a part, although whatever they granted to former soldiers was looked upon as a favor. The king gave pensions for services rendered, but these hardly ever affected anyone other than officers; outstanding action by common soldiers earned them only gratuities or sometimes jobs. The king reminded the monasteries and charitable institutions of their obligations and continued to send them soldiers. He granted gentlemen posts as administrators of the property of the abbeys, and he employed old soldiers to garrison the forts as *morte-payes*, or pensioners. All this could only affect a few hundred men, whose maintenance was often charged to the towns and who, discontented at the tedious lives they were forced to lead, often ran off to live as beggars.

In England, at the time of the Poor Laws of Elizabeth I, the acts of 1591, 1597, and 1601 instituted a system of pensions ranging from ten pounds sterling for common soldiers up to twenty for lieutenants. These amounts were raised, but the beneficiaries remained few.

In the meantime, several hospitals built to house disabled and elderly soldiers were opened throughout Europe. The earliest (if one excludes the Quinze-Vingts hospital for the blind in Paris) was founded by the king of Spain at Malines in 1585. Queen Christina of Sweden installed invalids in the Krigmanshus (hostel for military men) in Vodsterna in 1647. These establishments, however, could only take in a small number of pensioners.

After nearly a century of trial and error, a solution was reached in France with the founding of the Hôtel des Invalides. The idea goes back to the reign of Henry III. In 1576 Houel, a doctor, proposed founding in Paris a house for the poor, in which one section would be reserved for old soldiers. Henry IV made a short-lived attempt in 1604, founding in the Saint-Marcel district of Paris a charity house that was intended for poor gentlemen and disabled soldiers. Actually this move was directed largely toward resolving the many disputes among monasteries and their lay inhabitants, and recognizing the rights of the latter. The idea of a hostel for former soldiers was taken up by Richelieu in 1631 with the Commanderie de Saint Louis, and the government excused the monasteries from housing lay members, on payment of a pension equal to the cost of support. For lack of money, however, the Bicêtre hospital, designed to house a large number of old soldiers, was not finished, and the Thirty Years War and the Fronde made the need for a solution still more urgent.

In the middle of the seventeenth century, the great number of people living in misery led to both the charity campaign of Monsieur Vincent and the internment of the poor. Taking up

Richelieu's plans again, Louis XIV and Louvois succeeded in creating the Invalides (1670–1674); its first governor, significantly, was the provost general of the *bande*, that is, the highest authority in matters concerning discipline in the armies. Inmates were divided into three classes: officers, noncommissioned officers, and common soldiers. The last were forced to work at knitting stockings, and a rigorous discipline was imposed on all of the men, who were grouped into companies of subordinate officers and men. The invalids were soon too numerous to be kept together in the hostel. In 1690 those who were still capable of serving in sedentary positions were formed into detached companies of invalids, who were sent as garrison forces to forts throughout the kingdom.

At the close of the Seven Years War over 30,000 disabled soldiers were counted. Meanwhile the definition of "disabled" was enlarged, as progress was made toward recognition of a debt on the part of the State toward former soldiers, many of whom were still able to lead normal civilian lives. They married, sometimes without permission, and sought escape from military life. So admission to the Invalides was often converted into a pension paid to these veterans in their own homes. Twenty-five years of service qualified them for the equivalent of regular pay, and sixteen years for half-pay. A uniform was issued to them every eight years (*ordonnance* of 1764). From this time on there were three categories of ex-soldiers under the stewardship of the Invalides foundation: the badly disabled, who were kept at the hospital with the very old soldiers (whose numbers were reduced in 1776), the soldiers of the detached companies, and the pensioners.

In the early 1700s the problem of ex-soldiers was not the same throughout Europe. In Prussia the old soldier was a man who had lived at home nine or ten months out of the year, during peacetime, once his military training had been completed. He was less out of place in a society of an essentially military nature, and less apt to be without resources. In all countries, to some extent, companies of veterans were formed—sometimes fairly early, as in Spain—to man the garrisons. In the latter country from the seventeenth century on, gifts of 300 écus were promised to men who had undergone twenty years of active service, but when money was short these promises were unreliable. Sixty endowed positions were established in seaside towns for men over sixty years of age, twenty positions at twelve ducats a month, twenty at eight, and twenty at five. In Piedmont a deduction of two percent from the army's pay was made; in 1710 the disabled made up an autonomous corps in that area, and they were able fairly early to collect wages at home.

The problem of the maimed and crippled remained, to be solved largely along the lines of the French example. Foundations like the Invalides were created in England at Chelsea (1692); in Austria at Pest (1724), Vienna (1727), and Prague (1728); in Prussia at Berlin (1748); in Russia (1760); in Portugal at Runa (1792); in Sweden at Ulriksdal (1822). After 1717 invalids in Spain were divided into two groups, the "usable," who could carry out an auxiliary role, and the "completely useless," for whom a special establishment was created at Toro (Zamora province) in 1753. In contrast, Russia did not place the disabled in a single institution; monasteries had to take in crippled soldiers (1722), although in 1764 Catherine II took them out of the convents and distributed them among the towns.

We should add that several methods were used to take care of orphans. A discernible social policy toward the families of soldiers began to take shape in England, then in France in the late 1700s.

In the eighteenth century, States everywhere took over the whole problem, assuming the roles of the church, local bodies, and private foundations. Following the example of the French navy under Colbert, military administration, here as in other fields, generally led the way for civil administrations.

5

Military Nobility in the Service of the State

THE EXPRESSION *"noblesse militaire"* (military nobility or aristocracy), which appeared in France during the eighteenth century (specifically in an edict of 1750), would have been a redundancy in earlier centuries, since the nobleman's vocation had once been basically military. As the entire nobility did not in fact serve under arms, however, and as in the modern era many families were given noble rank for reasons other than military service, we will use the term to designate those of the nobility who actively served in the military professions. Rulers everywhere made attempts to place these aristocrats into the structures of the regular armies, to serve more or less permanently. Military service allowed noblemen to distinguish themselves in the eyes of the king and the court, and in public opinion generally; and as such service was closely bound up with relationships between State and society it is not surprising that there were as many different cases as countries. Nevertheless, the roles of the military nobility within the States roughly fell into three different categories. There were (1) countries like Poland, in which the State did not succeed in subjugating its military nobility, or those like Sweden, where the nobility, at first serving the State, later gained control over it; (2) Prussia, where the triumph of State policy led to a

87

militarization of the whole of the nobility and its almost complete incorporation into the army; and (3) countries like France, in which military service on the part of the nobility was not obligatory.

COUNTRIES IN WHICH THE NOBILITY REMAINED INDEPENDENT

There is no space here to expand on the general social evolution, but it must be remembered that the aristocracy in certain countries managed to avoid being "tamed" in the eighteenth century. The extreme example of this is, of course, Poland, where a gradual weakening of monarchical military institutions took place. Control of the troops slipped from the hands of the State, and State military archives, rich in material for the seventeenth century, are distressingly weak for the eighteenth. The royal army consisted of only a few companies and strongholds. After the reigns of Augustus II and Augustus III—the period of the "Saxon lethargy"—Stanislaus Poniatowski [Stanislaus II Augustus, king from 1764 to 1795] tried to make reforms; but he was unable to affect the military constitution of a country largely occupied by Russian armies. The national uprising led by Kosciusko was a brilliant spontaneous movement, but it was short-lived.

The example of Sweden is entirely different. The formation of a sizable national army under Gustavus Adolphus, as well as the openings provided for Swedish superior officers by the raising of troops in Germany, attracted a large proportion of the nobility to military service. The *Indelningsverket*, which involved great numbers of peasants, required a large permanent structure. And Charles XII appealed widely to the nobility during his campaigns. The latter agreed, therefore, to serve the State under arms, keeping a quasi-monopoly of the officers' positions. After the death of

Charles XII, however, they took revenge against the reforms of Charles XI, although in contrast to the Polish nobility they assumed domination over the State rather than simply destroying it. The *Riksdag*, in which the nobility held predominant power, controlled the *Indelningsverket*, and the constitution of 1720 granted the *Riksdag* the initiative in declaring war. Gustavus III was forced to carry out a coup d'état in order to re-establish the authority of the crown, in the process relinquishing the highest government posts to the nobility.

The evolution of the Hungarian aristocracy, although taking place within a very different context, was in some ways analogous to the Swedish process. The Hapsburgs could only hold on to this kingdom, reconquered from the Turks at the end of the seventeenth century, by allowing the magnates many important liberties. In 1765 Queen Maria Theresa tried to do away with the military obligations of the nobility, but the latter resisted, fearing the loss of their privileges as well, and the queen gave in. In Russia, military service by the aristocracy was not universal, but it was attended by important privileges. Noblemen were released from service to the State in 1762, but the authority of the sovereign remained undiminished.

MILITARIZATION OF THE PRUSSIAN NOBILITY

The kingdom of Prussia, an artificial State, was made up of distinct provinces situated mostly in that part of Germany east of the Elbe where great estates had been developing since the sixteenth century. The new *Rittergut* (knight's estate) usually combined earlier forms of seigniorial properties (*Gutsherrschaft* and *Grundsherrschaft*). These estates grew at the expense of the free peasants, and in the seventeenth century the landed nobility (the Junkers) maintained a very independent attitude toward the sovereign. When the Prussian kingdom was created in 1700, the regular army was regarded as a force that belonged to the sovereign rather than to the provinces or the State as a whole. The rural nobility in the Hohenzollern possessions looked on the army as a possible escape from poverty, but they felt in no way bound to serve. Moreover, many gentlemen went abroad to join foreign armies.

King Frederick William I, carrying out a policy comparable to that of Peter the Great in Russia, forced the nobility (except in the western provinces of Clèves and Juliers) to enter military service in behalf of a State of which he termed himself the foremost servant. The nobles had to agree in writing to serve, and they looked on this as forced labor rather than as a privilege. Every year each district (*Kreis*) had to furnish a specified number of young noblemen who were dedicated to military service. The ministries of Finance, War, and Lands notified the men who were qualified; the king decided which sons of which families were to enter the army; and the provincial councillor (*Landrat*) sent them to Berlin. Once there they could either enter cadet school or sign up with a regiment, in which they would become *enseignes* after two to four years.

This policy was a heavy burden on the nobility as a whole. Not only was the nobleman, like all other subjects, no longer allowed to serve abroad without being accused of treason, but he was not even allowed to leave the kingdom. Any unauthorized trip abroad meant the confiscation of his property. Even those nobles who went to foreign universities to study lost all chance of a position in Prussia. Certain activities were forbidden to the Junkers, particularly trade or contracting connected with royal property. In fact, the Junker was bound to his estate, which had to be kept up in order to provide officers for the king and sustenance for them: the estates became the economic base for the officers' corps. Laws of succession and inheritance in Brandenburg already required the consent of all male descendants for any transfer of a feudal estate, and Frederick William I strengthened them by requiring the sovereign's authorization for the sale of such estates. Frederick II encouraged the creation of entailed estates based on the rights of primogeniture, to avoid the splitting up of property.

The military obligations of the Junkers went still further. In contrast to the French nobles, who were exempt from the *taille* (a particular tax with a military origin), the Prussian nobles paid a military tax connected with the cavalry. The old taxation by fief (*Lehnritterpferdegeld*) was replaced by a system based on a fixed amount supposedly equal to the value of a horse, the *Geldkanon*; the amount was assigned by provinces. Nobles everywhere paid the *Kontribution* tax on their property, of course, even on estates in Prussia and Silesia.

In addition to taxes, military service itself was burdensome. Officers below the level of captain could not increase their low pay by profiteering, and they usually had to be supported by their families. An honest captain was little better off: to take charge of a company meant to take on the debts left by one's predecessor, and the nobleman who was both landowner and captain often had to leave the management of his estate to an administrator while he was away. The departure of any soldier meant the loss of a laborer for the estate—an especially unfortunate event if the seignior had had him trained for a trade. And a retired officer who became a provincial councillor was financially responsible for the affairs of the province.

The militarized Prussian nobility acquired a monopoly of the officer positions. In the judgment of Frederick William I, only aristocrats, endowed with a sense of honor, could serve properly as officers. Regulations for officers were different from those for noncommissioned officers or soldiers in the eighteenth century. Frederick II also preferred noblemen to the middle classes, although artillery and engineer branches (the *armes savantes*) did have officers of common backgrounds. But even here, in contrast to the practice in France, officers from the middle classes—never very numerous in any case—were fairly quickly given titles. Thus there was formed a professional order of officers, the *Berufstand*. Young noblemen were subjected to rigorous training. In 1739 the thirty-four generals in the Prussian army were all noblemen, as well as 200 of the 211 staff officers; there were no commoners listed among the captains or lower officers. In 1806, 695 commoners were found among 7,000 to 8,000 officers. Such a proportion was the more remarkable in that the number of men in active service in Prussia was high in proportion to the population and to the numerical importance of the aristocracy, while levies during times of war always brought still greater numbers of men of common background into the armies. In 1724 practically all adult noblemen were military officers or former officers. At the end of the eighteenth century the military nobility represented 68 percent of the aristocratic families in the electoral provinces and 60 percent of those in eastern Prussia, a proportion to be found nowhere else in Europe. Such a monopoly became a crushing expense, and to add to it the Junkers were forbidden to sell their estates to members of the middle classes. As compensation for these restrictions, all lawsuits being conducted against officers were suspended during the Seven Years War.

On the other hand, this monopoly meant that the Prussian nobility was considered to be the basic foundation of the State, and the king turned over to it considerable administrative and social power. The provincial councils, which together with the *Landrat* formed the highest administrative authority in the provinces, were made up of noblemen and especially officers, who were assumed to have had some training in army administration. The council portioned out the military responsibilities of the province. The Junkers were masters in the *Kanton*, and on their estates they carried out police and judicial functions. As captains they continually intervened in the lives of their vassals, reinforcing their baronial powers. Leaves of absence, resignations from the army, authorizations to marry—all depended on the captain. This strengthening of authority was similar to the evolution taking place in the rural society east of the Elbe, where forced labor was increasing and peasant-owned lands were shrinking. The peasant was becoming a worker, and the authority assumed by the landowning noblemen in the army was established over all peasants, whether in the army or not.

As we have seen, during the first half of the eighteenth century the nobility paid for this increasing power with heavy financial charges. The Seven Years War ruined many families and estates. But the situation changed in the last third of the century with the expansion of the rural economy in the countries of the East. The garrisons were markets, and the officers set the prices. Exports of wheat rose, and the grain-trading companies on the Elbe and the Oder included many officers among their shareholders.

Provisioning the companies could lead either to heavy expenses—for the negligent or the very conscientious—or to large profits. A captain received from the war fund a sum carefully calculated to support his company, and as in all eighteenth-century armies he was thus encouaged to manage his company like a business venture. He economized on uniforms, cut to minimum standards, and on minor details of equipment. Despite strict government control, embezzlement was common, all the more so because the company completely equipped itself: not until 1799 was even bread provided by the king. Captains demanded a fee before granting leaves or permission to marry, and another practice grew common in the Prussian army: the number of leaves and work permits granted far exceeded the authorized figure. If a soldier did not actually buy his permission for leave, he at least had to give up his wage to his captain. Work permits were common in the garrison towns, and men working temporarily outside their regiment were called *Freiwächter*. Their places had to be filled at the government's expense, and when general inspections were held the companies always counted extra men. This manipulation was so extensive that as an economic measure Frederick II kept in force the general

Grosse for recruits that he had instituted during the Seven Years War. The annual expenses for recruiting fell from 800,000 to 300,000 thalers.

The actual number of effectives was always well below the theoretical number. Frederick II could do no more than limit the extent of the problem. His successor made the situation official: captains were granted the right to keep the wages of fifteen *Freiwächter* per company. In wartime there were no *Freiwächter*, at least officially, but Frederick II agreed that compensation was due and he frequently distributed douceurs to the officers, according to rank.

Thus, despite appearances imposed by a rigorous governmental system, the Prussian companies had become enterprises with commercial value, and they "came up for sale" with every change in circumstances: at the end of the eighteenth century the price of a company rose to 2,000 thalers. It was especially those at the highest levels of the nobility and above the rank of colonel who profited. In addition, 800 monastic and collegiate prebends of over 2,000 thalers were distributed among these groups; in the final analysis, the nobility, though forced to serve, could draw some profit from the situation.

Maintaining such a large army put the sovereign in a dilemma: should he protect the peasants in order to be sure of a supply of recruits, or defend the estates and accord pre-eminence to the Junkers in order to insure a supply of loyal officers? Although measures were taken to support the peasants, like the edict of 1764 which prevented the confiscation of peasant landholdings by the nobility, the Prussian State in fact chose to protect its officers, that is, its noblemen. For example, the provincial governments formed credit institutions to help keep estates intact. In sum, then, although military service by the nobility was not required in the small western provinces, it led to serious social problems in all other areas.

Russia, already mentioned above, presents a modified version of the situation in Prussia. The seventeenth century had seen the progressive subjugation of the nobility to the State, in the framework of the *tchines*. The system was brought to its climax by Peter the Great, who also encouraged the westernization of his nobility. He allowed commoners, in theory, to aspire to the noble *tchines* in consideration of the functions which were now assigned to them. In the "century of empresses," the Russian nobility, like the Prussian nobility, gained moral and material advantages to balance the demands made upon them by the State. The peasants were left to their mercy, and they formed financial institutions for the purpose of preserving their estates. Eventually they were freed from service in 1762, but fondness for the autocratic monarch and the fact that distinction could only be acquired through service led many noblemen to remain in administrative and military positions. The officer corps were made up entirely of hereditary or newly created noblemen.

COUNTRIES IN WHICH THE
NOBILITY SERVED VOLUNTARILY

Voluntary military service by the nobility was the rule in most countries where a strong central government had arisen without claiming to control or change the moral structures of society. Two kinds of countries can be distinguished here. On the one hand, we find countries where fairly small armies required few officers and where other activities—intellectual, administrative, commercial, or maritime—kept the nobility occupied. Among these are most of the Italian states, Spain in the eighteenth century, and England. On the other hand, in states like France, Piedmont, and the German states except Prussia, large armies provided outlets for impoverished noblemen, and rulers encouraged them to serve.

Italian aristocrats had largely turned away from the profession of arms after the early sixteenth century, and those who persisted in military careers served abroad. In the seventeenth century there was very little military activity in the Italian states other than Venice and Piedmont (and that part of Italy controlled by Spain).

In England the gentry continued to control the militia, assuming this responsibility willingly since it carried a certain prestige. In the great economic expansion of the late seventeenth and eighteenth centuries, money joined land as a force to turn young gentlemen away from military preoccupations. Moreover, at no time except during the Civil War did the ruler maintain a large regular army. In the few English regiments in the English army the officers were noblemen by a large majority, but they were only a small fraction of the entire body of titled nobility. As the militia was only one of many activities of the gentry, not requiring their absence from their estates, we can say that notwithstanding the call to arms at the end of the eighteenth century military service to the State was not a serious burden except in wartime. Having given up the idea of maintaining a large army, the English rulers had no need to persuade the nobility to serve.

It was only in the second half of the eighteenth century that Spain, whose aristocrats were losing interest in warlike activities, joined this group of states. In this country military service by a large part of the nobility went back to the formation of the *tercios* in the early sixteenth century. There were many aristocrats on active duty under Philip II, and it was apparently not difficult for the rulers to find them because there were so many of them in the country. The prestige that accompanied army service even attracted the *letrados*, the scholars. Many of the hidalgos had little to do, and they were willing to become part of a strict military hierarchy in which ranks, duties, and honors were combined in various ways. An extremely detailed ordinance of 1632, regulating among other things the recruiting and promotion of officers, reveals a noteworthy advance over other countries at the time. Just as among the troops veterans were rewarded with higher pay (*ventajas*), among the officers distinction was made between *avantajados* and *entretenidos* at each level. The 1632 ordinance meant that the *ventaja* was not just a reward but also a kind of registration for those eligible for a higher rank. The minimum period spent at each of the lower ranks was firmly fixed: to become an *alferez* it was necessary to serve for six years, or four years in war; it took three years as *alferez* to become a captain. Above this rank advancement was by selection. The same ordinance, however, provided that these minimum periods could be reduced for men of illustrious ancestry to two years for *alferez* and six (instead of nine) for captain. We should note that the French army had no similar fixed rules for promotion until the second half of the eighteenth century.

The Spanish rulers could only require the nobility to go up through the ranks by granting in return a quasi-monopoly of the officers' positions. Even this did not keep them from becoming, like the rest of the population, weary of war. If we remember that in 1664 the *tercios* shrank to a few hundred, or even a few dozen, men, we can perceive that the 1632 ordinance could only have been weakly enforced. The rebirth of the Spanish army in the early eighteenth century did not lead to major conflicts between the State and the nobility. In fact, when the Spanish army ceased in the eighteenth century to be the army of a European empire and became a State (and colonial) army, military service was no longer required from a large proportion of the aristocracy. Even in Castile, which had provided so many military men in the sixteenth century, the ancient attraction to study and the absorption of scholars into administration tended to draw a large number of noblemen away from arms.

By contrast, in France, Piedmont, and the Hapsburg monarchy, the military policies of the rulers continued to make demands on the nobility. The evolution of relationships between the State and the military nobility in France is very complex. At several moments in the Wars of Religion or in the Fronde, one part of the military nobility ignored the demands of the State and attempted to create a situation like that which led Poland to its fate. On the other hand, under Louis XIV military service reached its highest point, and the progress made under the authority and the requirements of the French State undoubtedly influenced the projects of Peter the Great and Frederick William I. In any case, changes in French society in the eighteenth century confirmed the underlying trend toward noncompulsory military service on the part of the nobility, although the profession of arms continued up to the time of Voltaire to hold greater prestige within the ranks of the nobility in France than in England.

We must recall two facts that in the fifteenth and sixteenth centuries helped to shape the future of the French military nobility. First is the reinforcement of the distinction between the kind of military activity characteristic of the nobleman and that of the common man—a distinction made sharper by the constant calling up of the latter during times of war. It is true that military service on the part of the common man was no longer considered to be only temporary, but another gulf between the two kinds of fighting was established during the Hundred Years War: on the one side was the "warriors' war" of the nobles, who followed the rules of chivalry; and on the other was the "war to the death" waged by foot soldiers. To the first belonged all the virtues of war, in which the chevalier, true to his honor, followed a career filled with individual deeds that led to ever greater fame and glory. The knight Bayard was the model. In the second camp were found the common soldiers, who are generally called mercenaries, as if the nobility (excluding the "volunteers") fought without wages. Thus stereotypes were established that conformed to conceptions of society: gentlemen were granted places as officers, since service in the ranks was not conceivable for them, except perhaps in the king's household troops or in an elite corps, or again as "volunteers." Certainly in wartime this conception was weakened, but it came back in force with every "reform" (demobilization), particularly in 1559, 1598, and 1659.

The second fact is the practical distinction between the status of a nobleman and the profession of arms. Certainly the nobility continued to be the military order: the noble virtues were the warrior's virtues in the eyes of moralists up to the end of the eighteenth century. Nevertheless, arms was not the profession of many nobles, and a military career was not in itself enough to make one noble. In the seventeenth century we find few titles granted for military service alone. Most were given for other services or because the individuals lived like aristocrats, that is, they possessed revenues or responsibilities that allowed them to serve the State rather than work in other ways. Armed service in such cases added to the distinction of the family, but it was not absolutely necessary.

During the civil wars, a time when baroque elements were influencing French civilization, those nobles who sympathized with the several factions avoided serving the king, sometimes going so far as to raise their own troops or negotiate with foreigners. The nobility, particularly the military nobility, pursued personal goals. Power and reputation based on wealth, connections, and the King's favor were glorified, and an inflated conception of the nobleman's honor stimulated duels.

One cannot generalize, however. In the first half of the seventeenth century we see aristocrats who were magistrates, or who fulfilled other civil duties (*nobles de robe*), at the heads of bourgeois companies; and gentlemen were involved in all kinds of trafficking. Wars and political conflicts eroded the standards of the military nobility, who let themselves be contaminated by the behavior of the ordinary soldiers. Some went so far as to turn to highway robbery, like those condemned at the *Grands Jours* of Auvergne in 1665. Some of the aristocrats wore themselves out in useless political agitation. And, in spite of royal edicts that permitted the nobility to engage in commerce (except for "merchandising," or "keeping a shop"), prejudice against aristocrats in trade was so strong that they rarely engaged in it; the lesser nobility watched their wealth disappear rather than take economizing measures. Families who remained loyal to the king and who defended the State grew more powerful, however, and held onto their patrimonies.

After Richelieu, Louis XIV invited the nobility to work for the State, reserving his favor for those who served him well. The frequent wars rendered their military service even more important than before, as the nation undertook major military campaigns. Concerned with efficiency, Louis XIV attempted to limit the buying and selling of officers' posts. He opened the way upward through the ranks to the impoverished lesser nobility and even called upon commoners to command the increasing numbers of regiments. In 1664 the sale of positions was ended in the guard companies, except for the captains' posts. Lieutenant and lieutenant colonel positions became the basis for a *cursus* parallel to that for the venal captain and colonel positions. It had been impossible to take the step from lieutenant to lieutenant colonel without buying a post as captain and with it a company. Now one could get around the obstacle with the creation of the non-venal post of captain of grenadiers and the rank of "reformed" captain (this title was given to captains whose companies had been demobilized and was conferred now on an officer who had a captain's rank but no company). Also created were the functions of *aide-major* and major. Furthermore the rank of brigadier could be granted to both lieutenant colonels and colonels, and it allowed one to become a *maréchal de camp*, that is, a general officer. In these ways a gentleman without fortune could, at least in theory, rise to the highest positions in the army through his own worth and not because of purchased promotions.

Louis XIV demanded a great deal from his officers: physical sacrifices, reflected in the large numbers killed and wounded in battle, and spiritual sacrifices as well; the introduction of a more rigorous discipline under Louvois, who dismissed officers whose companies were badly run, caused trouble for many gentlemen. And, finally, there were financial sacrifices for a poor family buying a company for a son and obliged to support him while he was in the army.

On the other hand, Louis XIV gave tangible proofs of his favor. The *ordre du tableau* of 1675 instituting promotion by seniority allowed for the assignment of positions with less advantage accorded to high birth, and it permitted promotion for exceptional service. Pensions like the Order of Saint Lazare, admission to the Invalides, the granting of royal lieutenancies to retired officers, the creation of the Cross of Saint Louis in 1693—all these made possible some recompense while avoiding the promotion of men who were worthy but ill-fitted for superior offices. None of these rewards, incidentally, permitted commoners to enter the ranks of the nobility. In these ways Louis XIV attracted not only a large part of the French aristocracy but foreign noblemen as well, thus keeping up the numbers of his military nobility.

The wars of Louis XIV, however, exhausted the noblemen in the services, and money played an increasingly important part in their careers. In the first half of the eighteenth century, service became more and more costly because of the habits of the officers, who took many servants along with them on campaigns and entertained lavishly. Even captains had to keep up appearances. More serious was the fact that the route upward through the nonpurchasable positions was made very difficult by the prevalence of a certain arrangement called the *concordat*. At first, this was a matter of ensuring a sum of money to be paid to officers retiring from service. This sum, whose size varied according to the rank involved, was obtained by contributions from the officers of the corps, made either regularly or at the time of engagement. Although the *concordat* was strictly forbidden, it nevertheless persisted, and it led to a kind of business arrangement for all promotion within the regiment. For example, retirement by a lieutenant colonel led to a chain of promotions which meant that a replacement had to pay a certain sum to

whomever he replaced; and he was only partly compensated by
the amount given him by his own replacement. In 1714 the
Comte de Puységur wrote, "It is still true that there is hardly a
single captain whose position cost less than 6,000 livres; or a
captain of grenadiers who has paid less than 12,000 to 14,000
livres, including the *concordat* paid to those who were leaving; or
a lieutenant colonel who has given under 20,000 to 24,000 livres."
Access to these "nonpurchasable" positions was very expensive.

Nevertheless, the number of officers in the French army grew
very large. In 1775 the proportion of officers to men was one to
fifteen, with a total of no less than 1,100 colonels for 200 regiments, and 1,200 general officers. But in a society in which the
profession of arms no longer merited as much respect as in an
earlier period the nobility was becoming less interested in military
service. Army careers were less eagerly sought after, and 1,200 to
1,500 officers of less than fifty years of age left the army during
the Seven Years War. They were replaced by middle-class
bourgeois, actually men recently given noble rank, whose suit-
ability for military careers was—often wrongly—questioned.
Those noblemen who remained under arms were unquestionably
dedicated to the king's service, but they were only a part of the
nobility. Nine to ten thousand officers belonging to the hereditary nobility—perhaps 80 percent of the total—were in the
army. Adding to this retired officers, gentlemen serving as ordinary soldiers, and naval officers, we reach an approximate total of
20,000 to 25,000 gentlemen with military professions; at the most
one nobleman out of four was serving or had served in the king's
forces. Some, moreover, served for only a very short time, and
for many gentlemen a military career was no more than a potential outlet. In order to revive a military spirit within the nobility a
1750 edict announced the ennoblement of all general officers.
Similarly, in families in which three generations of officers had
obtained lifetime tax exemptions in return for length of service,
the third generation was created a member of the nobility pro-

vided he had received the Cross of Saint Louis. Commoners who fulfilled these conditions were actually very few.

It was generally assumed that the withdrawal of the nobility from armed service was partly responsible for the disasters of the Seven Years War. A debate began between the supporters of *la noblesse commerçante* and those of *la noblesse militaire*. (These were the titles of two works published a few months apart in 1756, by the Abbé Coyer and the Chevalier d'Arc.) Both hoped to help the nobility: the first would restore it through economic activity; and the second, on the side of the impoverished lesser nobility who appeared to be a source of virtue and valor, and inspired by the Prussian model, advocated a nobility based on military service, which would be open to commoners. The Baron de Bohan, in his *Examen critique du militaire français* (1781), gave his opinion that a special tax should be imposed on nobles who were not in the army. A generation of young officer-nobles, who were deeply humiliated by the defeat of Rossbach in 1757, and who admired Frederick II and his corps of officer-nobles, supported reforms proposed by Choiseul and Saint-Germain and were willing to pay the price of them. This meant, essentially, the taking over by the king of the regiments and companies in 1762 and the step-by-step suppression after 1776 of the selling of all military positions. A renewed military ethic was projected, raising sacrifice above outstanding feats of valor. It was the first sign of the ethic that was to be expressed in Vigny's *Servitude et grandeur militaires* [published in 1835]. The officers agreed, although sometimes reluctantly, to wear regimental uniform. The epaulette, called *"la guenille à Choiseul"* (Choiseul's rag), became the only distinctive sign of rank. Finally, although the cadet companies formed by Louvois could no longer be kept up after 1692, and another attempt to form them lasted only from 1726 to 1733, many young aristocrats now agreed to attend the military preparatory schools created in 1776 to supplement the Ecole Militaire founded in 1751. In the meantime, the minister Saint-

Germain reduced the number of officers: in 1789 there were 9,578. Only the nobility now had any real chance of promotion.

These reforms ensured that noblemen following military careers now became more professional, and at the same time they meant a rupture between those of the nobility who were in military professions and those who no longer were. Called for and adopted by the military nobility, the reforms were both a defense and a kind of rebellion, and they were to lead to a social and spiritual crisis in the army.

In Piedmont, rulers required a great deal from their nobility because of the large numbers of men kept on active duty. There, too, the rulers gave the nobility, in exchange, a quasi-monopoly of officers' posts.

In Austria the army had been bound to the dynastic rulers from the beginning, and some traces of this remained in the eighteenth century. The monarch's permanent army arose in the German states of the Hapsburgs. During the reign of Leopold I it went from 20,000 to 100,000, and commoners as well as noblemen of diverse origins were called upon to serve as officers for the regiments. According to Barker, at the time of the siege of Vienna in 1683, out of fifty-seven infantry regiments, twenty had colonels who were subjects of the Austrian Hapsburgs (among these were four Italo-Germans from the Tyrol and Styria and three Magyars); eight regiments were under non-subject Germans, six were under Italians, one was under a Scotsman, and one under a Pole. The families of twenty-nine of these colonels had served the Hapsburgs from before 1648; those of twenty others had joined the forces after that date; and eight colonels were from various ruling families of Europe. The struggle against the Turks (1683–1697, 1718–1722) and the Peace of Rastadt in 1714 brought Germans who were not subjects of the emperor, as well as other foreigners, into the Austrian army. Reorganized after 1715 by Prince Eugene and the Aulic Council of War, the army included Hungarian, Italian, and Walloon regiments. A certain mixing of elements took place among the officers, whose common motivation was their attachment first to the dynasty (for example, among the Lorrainers who had followed their duke, the future emperor, to Vienna), then to the Crown, finally to the State.

The number of foreign officers shrank during the eighteenth century, however. After the Seven Years War, and especially after the reign of Joseph II (1780–1790), the army grew more German in nature. Only the Hungarian and Walloon regiments retained their individuality, and German became the language of command. The nobility of all the states composing the Austrian monarchy adapted themselves to a more rigorous organization and discipline as the Austrian State, Vienna, and the court became increasingly important and attractive; serving the emperor (and king) conferred a new prestige in the eyes of the populace. We should add that the government, at least until Joseph II, made no systematic attempt to assimilate all noblemen into the German sphere. In a parallel evolution, the nobility found themselves gradually giving up their monopoly of officers' positions. Ultimately, reorganization into an immense territorial unit best served their own economic interests.

MILITARY INSTRUCTION OF THE NOBILITY

One indication that noblemen were tending to accept the idea of serving the State was the founding of military schools for them, although it must be admitted that implementation of plans for officer training by the State was slow and difficult.

According to the traditional pattern, the officer-noble not only underwent from childhood on an education that was of a military nature, but he actually learned the use of weapons, either in his own home or—for the wealthier—in an academy, before entering the army as a cadet serving an older relative. Academies had appeared in Italy in the sixteenth century, and from there they had spread throughout Europe. Pluvinel under Henry IV and Bernardi under Louis XIV were famous for the institutions they founded, and in the eighteenth century there were still several schools called "the king's academies." The academies were used mostly for the preparation of cavalry officers, as equitation was their principle subject. An "Ecole de Mars" was opened in 1738 by Lussan, who taught fortification. The prestige of the academies was dimmed somewhat in the eighteenth century in the face of progress in military arts. Royal pages or followers of great lords—for example, the pages at the Grande Ecurie (the stables) at Versailles—also received a kind of schooling through which they had good chances of receiving an officer's appointment.

The need for sound scientific knowledge was recognized early. La Noue mentioned this in 1587 in his *Discours politique et militaire*. The idea spread, especially in Protestant circles, and was taken up by the princes of Orange. Only a ruler had sufficient resources to undertake this kind of instruction. The first establishment that can be compared to a military school was probably the Académie des Exercices, founded in 1606 by the Duc de Bouillon, brother-in-law of Maurice of Orange, next to the Académie of Sedan. In 1617 John VII of Nassau founded the Kriegs und Ritterschule of Siegen. Maurice of Hesse founded the Kassel college in 1618, and Wallenstein opened military schools in Friedland and Gilschin. Richelieu founded an academy in the Temple district in Paris where surveying and drawing of plans, a little history, and some geography were taught. The Duke d'Enghien, the future victor at Rocroi, studied there in 1637. Wars, however, destroyed these first efforts.

Theoretical military instruction did not cease, for meanwhile the Jesuit and Protestant colleges were including mathematics and fortification among their courses. It may have been the Great Elector who thought to gather the cadets scattered among the regiments into one company stationed near the Ritterakademie of Kolberg. Cadet companies multiplied in several countries, but their survival was often precarious because of lack of money. In

Prussia some were attached to older regiments quite early. Louvois took up the Great Elector's idea in 1682, creating nine companies of 400 to 420 men quartered in strongholds, but financial difficulty forced him to abandon this in 1696. A new, more modest attempt was made in 1726, in six garrisons with companies of 150, but it too was given up in 1733. The cadet company organized for colonial service was more fortunate; it lasted at Rochefort from 1730 to 1789.

The State by no means abandoned all interest in the training of future officers. Certain corps served as "nurseries" for army staff. In France there were the king's regiment (1663), the corps or companies of the king's household (the musketeers and above all, after 1664, the bodyguards), and the gardes françaises, after 1716. In Russia the Préobrajensky and Semonovsky regiments at St. Petersburg fulfilled a similar role; Peter the Great insisted that aristocratic families send their sons to these regiments.

A more complex problem faced the artillery and engineers branches, which were attracting those of the lesser nobility who were not too poor, and the middle classes. In the western countries, in addition to receiving instruction in the colleges, engineers and artillery officers served an apprenticeship under the best-known technicians. In the seventeenth century many engineers went to Italy, Holland, then France to study. In Russia nearly everything still remained to be done in this field by the eighteenth century. Peter the Great established artillery schools in 1701, engineering schools (1709), and schools of military medicine (1707). An artillery school was attached to the Royal Cannoneers in France after 1679; in 1719 and again in 1756 a special school of fixed artillery was attempted at La Fère, then at Bapaume, but the pattern of schools attached to each battalion (1722) or each artillery regiment (1772) was preferred. In contrast to most of these, the Ecole de Mézières, opened in 1749, centralized the training of engineers. In England artillery officers and engineers were trained at Woolwich after 1741.

The idea of schools for future officers spread from the artillery and engineers branches to other branches, for although a certain number of officers had an extensive classical education, many could barely read and write, a situation that became increasingly difficult. In 1720 Frederick William I brought the Prussian cadet companies together into a school for cadets at Stolpe, then Potsdam, Kulm, and finally Berlin. Others followed this lead, particularly in Russia with a corps of aristocrat-cadets (1730), and in Saxony with a school at Dresden.

Louis XV, urged by Madame de Pompadour and Pâris-Duverney, founded the Ecole Royale Militaire for five hundred young gentlemen. This grandiose institution accomplished more in assisting impoverished aristocrats than in providing a solid training for future officers, for the disparity in the ages and levels of education of the students was too great. In 1776 Saint-Germain founded twelve military schools, at La Flèche (which since the expulsion of the Jesuits had already been serving as one), at Sorèze, Brienne, Auxerre, and elsewhere. The best students, selected by examination, entered the gentleman-cadet corps at the Ecole Militaire in Paris, until it was suppressed in 1788. Schools of this sort were created in Austria (at Wiener-Neustadt in 1752, where students were prepared by the Thérésianum installed at the castle of La Favorite), in St. Petersburg, in Munich, in Naples, at Sandhurst in England (1799), and elsewhere.

The training of infantry officers during the eighteenth century actually owed little to the schools, but nevertheless one consequence of their formation was that little by little the military nobility undertook some study. In passing through the cadet companies or the schools, furthermore, they were molded to a common pattern, which by the end of the eighteenth century was under the control of the State.

In the eighteenth century, then, a part of the European aristocracy, more or less powerful according to country, underwent a discipline that was no longer questioned, although it may not always have been accepted eagerly; and the nobles had gained in exchange a near-monopoly of officers' positions. Furthermore, in the eastern countries the aristocracy had strengthened its power, which was based on landownership, and profited from the growth of serfdom. However, the demands made by the governments now frequently added urgency to the need for training imposed by the evolving military arts, and a gentleman's upbringing was no longer adequate training for an officer. Officers' corps became more professional everywhere. Outside of Prussia, where a military career had always been respected throughout the whole of society, and other countries where its prestige had remained high, the new professionalization of the officers' corps meant that the military nobility now stood out from the rest of the nobility; their way of life, their behavior, and their attitudes distinguished them, although they were not isolated on the level of social relationships, nor in the general effort to defend the aristocratic order. The situation was difficult and complex for those who were controlling the destinies of the States.

6

Militarily Dominated States and States with Civilian Emphasis in the Eighteenth Century

POLITICAL CIRCUMSTANCES were now strongly influencing the degree of importance assumed by military affairs. For example, although the sovereign did not necessarily desire it, colonial settlements prepared themselves for military action, particularly in French Canada. In Europe the status of the army within each State was largely determined by the governments as soon as they had managed to subdue the nobility politically. Yet we must not forget several points: the "State" was a recent concept, and one which individuals resisted for a long time; management of its economic affairs was difficult; the traditions of provincial and regimental autonomy were still powerful; and the States in general saw themselves as preservers of existing family and social values.

We can approach the question of the status of the armies within the States by comparing the military endeavors of the different governments. And it will be still more worthwhile to investigate the effects of these military efforts on the formation of the governments themselves. This will allow us to distinguish between a completely military state like Prussia, the states in which military matters predominated (for the most part in eastern

Europe), and those with an increasingly civilian character (principally in western Europe).

THE EXTENT OF MILITARY EFFORT

An attempt can be made to compare military efforts quantitatively by determining the proportions of military expenses within budgets, the proportions of men in military service within entire populations, and—in relation to the question of the importance of the role of the nobility within the State—the proportions of officers within the total numbers of aristocrats.

To evaluate military budgets is extremely difficult, even for the late eighteenth century. Notwithstanding a general similarity of military institutions, troop expenses were covered by appropriations in tax money or in kind, arrangements too diverse to be compared at all precisely.

In certain countries we see tax money specifically destined for troop support, like the original *taillon* in France. This was particularly true in Prussia, with its direct taxes (the *Kriegskontribution* paid by the peasants, the *Kavalleriegeld* (paid by the townsmen and countrymen), and indirect taxes (the *Kriegsmetzkorngeld*, paid on the grain harvest). In addition, the coffers of the *Marsch und Molestien*, whose purpose was to repay peasants for damage caused by the army, were supplied by a tax (the *Kriegsfuhrgeld*), so that the peasants largely paid for their own compensation.

Or money for troop support could be taken from general taxes: in Prussia, the *accise* on merchandise, in France, the *taille*, the *capitation*, the *vingtième*. And it must be remembered that military taxes in money did not preclude contributions in kind, such as providing convoy support, maintaining militias, housing soldiers; these were sometimes converted into taxes, but they were informally levied and often difficult to evaluate. It would also be essential to take into account the fiscal systems, allowances for exemptions, and economic programs of each country, in assessing the actual burden of military expenses on the citizens.

According to Otto Büsch, military costs in Prussia rose to two-thirds of the State expenses. In 1787 military expenditure for regular troops alone would have been around 101,500,000 livres in France, 74,200,000 in Austria, and 44,000,000 in Prussia, to supply comparable numbers of effectives. Piedmont appears to have been a state in which military expenses were among the highest in Europe. Guido Quazza reports that military expenditure probably reached 54.2 percent of the total expenditure in the years of peace from 1720 to 1733, and 68.1 percent in the period from 1734 to 1740, three years of which were war years. In the last years of the ancien regime in France, military expenditures rose to 30 percent (20 percent for the land army). The Spain of Charles III is revealed as more parsimonious: in 1771 half the infantry was disbanded for four months in an economy measure.

We can also attempt to classify the governments by considering the relationships of numbers of men on active duty to whole populations, figures that shed light on the programs and intentions of the rulers. Such an analysis produces the following table. This kind of table can only be approximate, as the real number of men in service is always lower than the theoretical number; and the population figures are not universally accepted, either. Also, the separate groups of militiamen who were not incorporated into regular units must be added (in France, for example, this could be as many as 100,000 men), not to mention naval forces. And finally, it is necessary, for some countries, to take into account foreign recruiting, in order to obtain an accurate assessment of the relationship of the entire population to servicemen of national origin—in other words, of the pressure of recruiting on the populace. This is particularly true for Great Britain, Sweden in 1709, Prussia, and France.

An accurate count of foreign soldiers within a country is far from simple because of the many kinds of deception practiced. False identities were used in both native and foreign regiments,

TABLE 1
Effectives in the Regular Armies and Populations of the States

State	Date	Effectives	Population[a]	Ratio of Effectives to Population
Austria	1705	100,000	8,000,000	1/80
(Hapsburg States)	1786	240,000[b]	23,000,000	1/96
France	1710	300,000	20,000,000	1/66
	1738	140,000	22,000,000	1/157
	1760	280,000	24,000,000	1/86
	1789	180,000	26,000,000	1/144
Great Britain	1698	24,000	10,000,000	1/416
and Ireland	1710	75,000	11,000,000	1/147
	1747	120,000	12,000,000	1/100
	1783	51,000	16,000,000	1/314
Piedmont	1734	43,000 (incl. militia)	2,300,000	1/53
	1738	30,000	2,300,000	1/77
Prussia	1740	80,000	2,200,000	1/28
	1760	260,000	3,600,000	1/14
	1786	194,000	5,700,000	1/29
Russia	Beginning of 18th century	220,000	14,000,000 (?)	1/64
	1796	300,000	36,000,000	1/120
Spain	1759	56,000	9,000,000	1/161
Sweden	End of 17th century	40,000	1,000,000	1/25
	1709	110,000	1,400,000	1/13
	End of 18th century	45,000	2,000,000	1/44

[a]From M. Reinhard, A. Armengaud, and J. Dupaquier, *Historie de la population mondiale*, 3d ed. (Paris, 1968); and P. Léon, *Economies et sociétés préindustrielles*, vol. 2, 1650–1780 (Paris, 1970).
[b]Including about 35,000 Hungarian soldiers and 15,000 from the "national regiments" of the Austrian Netherlands. To this figure must be added 72,000 from the *confins militaires*, according to Archives de la Guerre (Paris), A-1, 3766, p. 94.

and inversely native soldiers were to be found in "foreign" regiments. One illustration is the German-speaking men of Alsace and Lorraine, who made up about one-third of the "German" regiments in the French army in the second half of the eighteenth century. Soldiers of foreign origin enrolled in the French army in peacetime represented about one-eighth of the total, and in wartime, about three-fourths. In the native regiments of the Austrian Netherlands, foreign recruitment (according to J. Ruwet) was about 17 percent in 1750, nearly one-fifth in 1770, and more than one-fourth in 1786–1787. Such a pattern, incidentally, appears to be peculiar to the Austrian Netherlands. In general, the growing national sentiment became increasingly opposed to the idea of service in foreign armies. We know of course that England used fairly large numbers of German regiments, and that there were few armies that did not include foreign units (Walloon guards in Spain, regiments of French deserters in Prussia, Swiss regiments nearly everywhere, and so on), but we do not know the exact proportions of native to foreign servicemen. The table does, however, allow us to pick out states with fairly low recruiting ratios, like England or Spain. The mean appears to be a little under one soldier for each one hundred inhabitants.

As to the second table, which concerns the role of military service in the activities of the nobility, it too is only an approximate indication; the proportions of nobles in the officers' corps of the different countries, as well as the actual numbers of noblemen, are not known precisely. It is clear that where aristocrats existed in great numbers (Spain, Hungary, Russia) the number of them who were in military service was relatively low. We should also have to take into account the navies, which attracted many noblemen in France and England; the gentlemen who served among the troops; and finally the fact that in some countries, like France, gentlemen served for relatively short periods. Including navy figures, perhaps one nobleman out of five bore arms. The table is useful, however, for the pressure

TABLE 2
Number of Officers and Nobles in the Different States

State	Date	Approximate Number of Officers	Approximate Number of Nobles[a]	Ratio of Officers to Nobles
Austria	End of 18th century	5,000-6,000[b]	90,000	1/15-1/18
France	1775	12,000[c]	400,000	1/33
	1789	10,500	400,000	1/38
Great Britain and Ireland	1783	2,000(?)	50,000-75,000	1/25-1/38
Hungary	End of 18th century	2,000-4,000	400,000	1/100-1/200
Piedmont	Middle of 18th century	1,600-2,000	25,000(?)	1/13-1/16
Prussia	1740	3,100	22,000	1/7
	1786	5,500[d]	57,000	1/10
Russia	End of 18th century	12,000	600,000	1/50
Spain	End of 18th century	2,400	400,000	1/167
Sweden	1757	1,400	10,000-15,000	1/7-1/11(?)

[a]From J. Meyer, *Noblesses et pouvoirs dans l'Europe d'Ancien Régime* (Paris, 1973).
[b]Including 124 general officers in 1787 (Archives de la Guerre, Paris, A-1, 3766).
[c]Including 779 general officers in 1787 (*ibid.*).
[d]Including 103 general officers in 1787 (*ibid.*).

brought to bear on the nobility to serve affected their attitudes toward arms and military activity. Rulers could not ignore this fact.

A MILITARY STATE: THE KINGDOM OF PRUSSIA

The tenth largest State in Europe in area and the thirteenth in population at the end of the eighteenth century, Prussia had the third or fourth largest army in terms of number of men. Nowhere else was there a similar percentage of subjects in uniform, and nowhere else did the army demand so much from all citizens. The creation of the *Kantonsystem* in 1733 changed the very nature of the provinces, as the canton quickly became the fundamental unit of the State, on which depended the welfare of society and the government (see O. Büsch). Citizens were bound to their canton: to prevent an exchange of recruits or enlistees a man was forbidden to leave his own district, and no one could move into a canton without authorization from its governing officer. It became the intermediate administrative mechanism between the authority of the State, represented by the *Landrat*, and the local manorial estate.

Such a situation meant hardships for everyone. After a training period of one and a half or two years, the Kantonist could hope to live at home for nine or ten months out of the year, in contrast to soldiers in other countries; but unlike the militiaman he continued to be a regular soldier, under the command of his captain. Frederick II reviewed his troops once a year, and as he could not do this for the entire army all at the same time the reviews were spread throughout most of the year, often coinciding with periods when agricultural workers were needed on the farms. The Kantonist had always to wear some of his equipment in the village, and on Sundays he had to attend service in full uniform. These requirements affected even the *Obligats*, the boys who were enrolled at ten years old, who had to wear some distinctive emblem (usually a red scarf) and attend periodic meetings called by a regimental officer. All who had been enrolled were answerable to regimental tribunals for any desertion, that is, trip out of the canton. Eventually, as soldiers were supposed to sell their old uniforms every year, many peasants bought these clothes and dressed themselves in bits of military clothing.

Within the system of royal ordinances the captain had become the ruler of the canton. He could interfere in an individual's private affairs and influence the lives of whole families. It was he who selected recruits from among the *Obligats*, and in his search for tall men an officer sometimes turned to those who were exempted from service. As in all armies, a soldier needed official authorization to marry; in Prussia this was not simply a formality and, as we have seen, some captains were not above selling such authorizations. An officer might even intervene in arrangements of legacies so that the son who was the smallest or the least fit for service would inherit the family farm. Contrary to rules, some captains claimed the same rights over men who had enlisted. It is easy to understand why, whenever possible, peasants chose to take over poor farms as *Kossäte* [see p. 59] in order to avoid military service. Such conditions eventually gave a new militaristic character to the seigniorial regime. Enforcement of military discipline after the Seven Years War had repercussions on the estates, where the baron disciplined his peasants just as he punished his soldiers in the army.

It should be noted that military service had contrary effects as well. First of all, officers, who were aware of the need to give the peasants enough liberty and prosperity to bear the expenses that the low wages did not cover, were inclined to defend the peasants' property rights against the claims of the great estate-owners. Such control did not exist in the areas east of the Elbe, where the powerful aristocracy continued to enlarge their properties. And there were other results. In a country that was becoming increasingly military in character, the Kantonist sensed his importance. For some, the time spent at home was a holiday leave rather than time granted for working on the farm. The Kantonist could sometimes count on the military courts to oppose the abuses of the *Landrat* or the lords of the estates. He felt that military service made him a direct vassal of the king and that consequently such service might free him from baronial rule. In fact, this did happen in the royal domains in 1777, and later, in 1807, in the rest of the country.

The army thus pervaded the entire life and structure of the Prussian kingdom. We have seen that conflicts in which civilians and military administrators were opposed were judged by mixed tribunals where military men held the most important places. The bureaucracy was partly designed to serve the army, for example, in the War and Land departments. Retired military men held many posts as ministers, directors of Finance, War, and Land departments, in provincial governments, as advisers, directors, presidents, treasurers, inspectors, postmasters, forest wardens, and so forth. Such a preponderance of military elements in civil administration was reinforced by family alliances and connections. And the whole economy was affected by the presence of a large army. A garrison was a market in which officers controlled the prices of food supplies and the local taxes on such supplies. Construction of barracks employed, besides soldiers, the *Freiwächter*, who furnished hand labor for the village craftsmen. Even colonization of new areas was related to the army: although the kings exempted colonists from service in order to attract them to the colonies, it has been estimated that the army secured for the kingdom 300,000 to 400,000 new subjects, former soldiers of foreign origin who settled as colonists during the eighteenth century. To some of them the king granted farms that had been abandoned in wartime, especially in annexed areas. In terms of social relationships this permeation by military elements meant the firm establishment of military men in the midst of civilian populations.

STATES IN WHICH MILITARY
AUTHORITY PREDOMINATED

Let us look now at the states that were not completely militarized, as was Prussia, but in which a military influence was perceptible in civil bureaucracies, in economic matters, and in personal relationships. While officers everywhere were linked to the nobility, soldiers either remained closely connected to their popular origins, as in Sweden, or in contrast were deliberately removed from them, as in Russia. The Hapsburg monarchy is a complex case, as is to be expected from the diversity of the countries within it.

In Sweden the system of the *Indelningsverket*, although hampered by a certain rigidity in the eighteenth century, was to mark rural society permanently. The geographical boundaries of the military recruiting regions remained in existence up to recent years, and the groups of peasants (*rotar*) who supplied and supported one soldier each maintained a degree of identity. The routes that crisscrossed the countryside, linking military centers and giving access to ports, were very useful to the economy. The system itself, however, was not an economic advantage; it suited a country in which the heavy copper currency was an inconvenient means of exchange: fiscal demands were fewer because of the shift of some of the responsibility for troop support directly to the peasants. The *Indelningsverket* tended to strengthen local economic affairs at the expense of a broader exchange economy, and it is blamed for the failure of the economic reforms initiated by Gustavus Adolphus and Oxenstierna in the seventeenth century.

These disadvantages were slowly overcome. First of all, although the population grew, the number of effectives remained stationary. Thus the cost of maintaining the army was, relatively, reduced. The *Indelningsverket* resulted in a consolidation of the position of the landed nobility, and the latter slowly began to engage in commercial activities. They took an active part in politics as well, throughout the eighteenth century, and as their activities were broadened the military character of the State in which they were playing a leading role was somewhat diminished. Another consequence was that the Swedish army, apart from the royal guard and the artillery, was no longer precisely a professional army. If the soldier, who lived in his village except in wartime, was set somewhat apart from rural society, he still maintained close and continuous relationships with the peasants of the *rotar*. At both levels—officers and men—the Swedish army maintained contact with the civilian population.

The situation was entirely different in Russia, where the two levels have to be treated distinctly. Officers belonged to the *tchines* and were usually the sons of *tchinovniki*. Their recruitment was in fact similar to that of Prussian officers. We have noted that the release from obligatory State service, granted to the nobility in 1762, apparently had little effect on the army. Moreover, all administrators, civil as well as military, were bound by the same military discipline, which became even stronger after the Seven Years War, as it had in Prussia. At the end of the eighteenth century the *tchinovniki* were wearing uniforms, and military values became very important in the aristocratic ethic and in the orientation of the whole Russian State.

Matters were different among the masses, outside of the eastern border areas. Setting aside the Cossacks, who were militarily organized, the region of the Urals included several fortified outposts, kernels of future towns, responsible for defending settlers, mines, and routes against raids from the Bashkirs and the Tatars. The towns were like camps, and a kind of military discipline was imposed on the miners and ironworkers. It was in this region, incidentally, that the Pugachev revolt (1773–1774) began. After that, the government made sure that the inhabitants were not armed. In the rest of the empire the army, housed in military barracks quite early, was a largely urban institution, somewhat isolated from the peasants. Although most countrymen were affected by conscription to some extent, it actually took only a little over three percent of the male adult population. And a soldier remained in the army for his entire life, spending his old age in veteran companies. The length of service was not limited to twenty-five years until the end of the century. A soldier seems to have had some hope of advancement throughout most of the century—for example, by entering the elite regiments stationed in St. Petersburg; but by the late 1700s a rise from the ranks to officer status had become more difficult. The soldier was thus simply taken away from his village, and except for the officers, the army was cut off from the civilian population.

The Austrian monarchy provides an extraordinary range of roles possible for an army within a State. We find areas that were militarily organized—the *confins militaires* on all the frontiers with the Ottoman Empire. They had been settled by soldiers who had been granted land as wages, and they were divided into regimental regions, in turn grouped into company cantons according to a system similar to the *Indelta*. Administration was carried out by officers under the authority of the commanding generals of Croatia and Slavonia (ten regions), the Banat and Serbia (five regions). In all, the hussar regiment and the sixteen infantry regiments of the *confins* included 72,000 men in 1787, of whom only one-third could be called away to other theaters of operation. They received wages only in wartime.

The Milan district presents an example of a state with great strategic importance; the Austrian troops, stationed in the capital and in the forts of the defensive quadrangle, were foreigners. The Austrian Netherlands had a government that was predominantly civilian, and the troops were largely recruited within the country and commanded by native officers. All promotion for aristocrats in the army depended on Vienna. It is to be noted that military influence was stronger in the provinces east of the Liège diocese than in the richer central or western districts.

In the Hereditary States the nobility had freely entered into military service when Leopold I and Prince Eugène had created a large Austrian army. After the appeal made in 1740 to the Hungarian nobility by Maria Theresa, they too followed suit. For Bohemian nobility, after the Battle of White Mountain, and for the Polish nobility of Galicia, annexed in 1774, service in the Austrian army was a means of demonstrating their loyalty and gaining favor at the Viennese court. It is generally agreed that in the nineteenth century the army was a centralizing force for the Danubian monarchy as well as an instrument for Germanization, and thus one of the strongest foundations of the State. By 1740 twelve infantry regiments out of fifty-two, and twenty-five cavalry regiments out of forty, were already stationed in Hungary, and many of them were not Hungarian recruits.

It was under Maria Theresa that the army took on the centralizing role and acquired new prestige in the State. The empress had medals struck on which she was portrayed as *Mater castrorum*. Officers were declared *hoffähig*, that is, they could be presented at court in uniform. The War Commissariat created by Haugwitz in 1749 began the reduction of the military autonomy of different areas of the monarchy, and the trend continued under Joseph II. As regiments were still characteristically recruited within separate provinces, the mixing of men of diverse origins took place primarily at the officer level. The military nobility were not cut off from the rest of the aristocracy, but the troops were ofter uprooted by service in garrisons far from their native regions.

The one characteristic common to all the countries in which military aspects were dominant, except certain parts of the Austrian monarchy, was the presence of a weak bourgeoisie, or urban middle class. A powerful nobility was the trump card with which a monarch could maintain the military character of his State.

STATES IN WHICH CIVIL
AUTHORITY PREDOMINATED

In western Europe the lowered public esteem for arms that stemmed, on the one hand, from an evolution in economic activity and from the "new spirit" and "enlightened" philosophy and, on the other hand, from the progress in military arts led in general to a pronounced professionalism among military men and a growing distinction between them and civilians. It followed that military authority was less pronounced over civilians now protected by civil agents like the French intendants from abuses by the troops. Governors of provinces (the lord-lieutenants in England) and of fortified areas continued to be military men, but they seldom displayed their military status except when they presided at certain ceremonies and when they took part in maintaining public order, for they controlled armed forces. The growth of parliamentary power in England and the development of administration by intendants in France signalized the increasing predominance of civil power. The formation of war secretariats or councils gradually brought about a reorganization of all army affairs within governments.

Distinctions must be recognized, however. Whenever it was considered necessary, military men continued to fill important roles, as in frontier regions, fortified areas, military ports, and colonies.

After the two revolutions in England, that country could no longer maintain a military character. In the eighteenth century the army seemed to be little connected with the nation, and even rather foreign to it as it existed early in the Hanoverian dynasty, up to the Seven Years War. Regiments were for the most part stationed in Ireland, on the continent, or in the colonies. The few troops in Great Britain itself were scattered throughout the towns, but the soldiers were looked on as strangers by the inhabitants. Officers were more and more apt to come from certain families. Such isolation was increased by confinement in barracks and severe discipline. Articles of war and mutiny edicts were constantly being issued and rewritten in great detail. Wearing uniform became obligatory in 1742 (red for the line army, blue for troops under the authority of the Ordnance Board). The number of effectives fluctuated widely. Down to 24,000 in 1698, only 7,000 of which were in Great Britain, it reached 75,000 during the War of the Spanish Succession and 120,000 in 1747 (of whom many, it is true, were foreign soldiers). In peacetime the army was held to about 45,000 men. In 1783 there were recorded 18,500 stationed in Great Britain, 12,500 in Ireland, 13,000 in the colonies, and 7,000 in India. After the sixteenth century the defense of Great Britain against a possible invader was evidently left to the fleet and the militia; the latter became, in spite of appearances, increasingly professional, although it lacked the prestige of the regular armies. The habit of the kings—theoretical heads of the army—of wearing uniform although they had been forced to give up real power to a cabinet responsible to Parliament, provides an intriguing symbol of the isolation of the army within the nation.

In France the situation was more complicated. Ties between civil and military administrations remained strong. The War Secretariat was still given responsibility for ordinary communications between the court and most frontiers, while Paris and other general areas were left to the committees of the king's household, which gradually became the equivalent of an Interior Ministry. The intendants continued to assume responsibility for troop support and to control the militias. On the other hand, after the appointment of Marshal de Belle-Isle to the War Secretariat, the war ministers were military men, and the administration of the army assumed a more military nature. This held true for commissioners, comptrollers, and army inspectors, whose numbers multiplied.

The changes that took place in the army at the end of the

eighteenth century were the work of military men entirely, in contrast to what had happened under Louis XIV. The War Council formed in 1788, which decided almost independently all matters affecting the army, was made up of officers of general rank. We have seen that the professionalism of the officers' corps was intensified by the military schools; the creation of the first schools for children of military personnel under Louis XVI, and the wearing of uniform by the officers, were part of the same trend. Soldiers were increasingly isolated from civilians as barracks housing grew. Military housing was not yet universal, and it was not to be completely achieved until the property of the church was transferred to the nation, a process that made available a great number of abbeys that could easily be transformed into barracks. The army became in some ways increasingly isolated within a State that was becoming more and more civilian-oriented. The court at Versailles had never had a military aspect, but the sovereign had considered himself to be the head of his armies. Louis XVI not only did not cultivate any military mannerisms, which were now out of fashion, but he did not even wear a uniform.

It is true that ten years after the fall of the ancien regime a political regime of a decidedly military character was installed. The revolution that made this possible (unexpected as it may have been in 1789) and Bonaparte's ambition were not the only reasons. There still existed in France certain elements that favored the establishment of a military State. There was first of all the idea of military duty that awoke whenever there was need. Strangely enough, this was illustrated in New France, where, in order to survive, society took on a military character, and where the predominance of military men steadily grew. The militia was in constant action there from 1691 on, and in 1760 nearly all able men had campaigned at least once. The army and the navy absorbed a third of the adult males, according to W. J. Eccles. Most of the nobles served as officers, in the independent naval companies stationed in Canada as well as in the militia. The military establishments—the forts and garrisons—were major economic factors, and the colonial government and local administrations were military in nature. Thus the militia captain was a police officer, and the intendant arrested criminals at his order. A military ethic that included aristocratic values dominated the colonies, and such a character was to last into the early years of English rule. We should remember that, when they left Europe, future Canadians were no different from other Frenchmen.

Military influence was very strong in the frontier provinces of the north and east, particularly in Lorraine—a fairly poor country where fortified camps meant a powerful military apparatus, a market, and employment. It is interesting to note that the frontier regions of France were usually republican in their sympathies, and later supported the Empire. Throughout the kingdom, appeals for troops to suppress uprisings—relatively rare under Louis XV—increased toward the end of the ancien regime. Soldiers were not looked upon as palace guards or political agents, and some town corps, like that of Le Havre, asked that troops be used to free the bourgeois-militiamen from the duties of the night watch. The military insurrections of 1790 encountered a sympathetic response among civilians, especially among former soldiers who were living on pensions as civilians. With the Revolution, the State ceased to be the intermediary between the army and society that it had become by the late eighteenth century. These two forces re-established direct contact without any difficulty.

In Bourbon Spain, as in France, the army turned in on itself, especially during the reign of Charles III. The House of Savoy, which gave a great deal of attention to its army, nevertheless was not able or did not wish to turn Piedmont into a military state.

In all the European countries technical progress in the military arts tended to create a specialized role for the armies and to isolate the soldiers. While officers set the style for government administrations in the East, this was not true in the West, where they often chose to retreat into their profession and associate only with their own fellow-officers. There is no question that the existence of a powerful middle class in England and France helped to direct the State toward a civil rather than a military emphasis. But was this the case in Spain and Piedmont? It appears that the nature of the nobility was crucial. Less exclusively devoted to the exploitation of their estates, more urban, often of ecclesiastical backgrounds, less arrogant and readier to associate with the middle class—especially in England—the nobility allowed the State to adopt a progressively less military character. We can safely assert that it is in those States that emerged early from medieval social conditions, and where the new attitudes were shared by more than the sovereign and a small elite, that the predominance of civil power is first evident. In contrast, the more military States at the end of the eighteenth century are those where monarchs were imitating the statism of Louis XIV and practicing "enlightened despotism."

PART III

Military Society

The distinction between the military profession and military obligation led to the formation of a military society within the wider society and more or less isolated from it. While remaining linked in many ways to the whole of society, military society nevertheless exhibited enough special characteristics to be considered a separate "order" comparable to the clergy. Like the latter, the army was not a social but a vocational order, and a judicial one as well, possessing its own laws. Again like the clergy, it was divided into two sub-orders, linked by a common purpose: officers and common soldiers were the respective counterparts of the high and the low clergy. In both cases the subdivisions tended to reflect the two great social orders—noble and common—and promotion from the lower rank to the higher was not easy. In contrast to the clergy, however, a common purpose did not bring about an entirely common ethic. While moralists endow the officer with a sense of honor inherited from the days of chivalry, they have often tended to see the soldier as nothing but a social reject, representing the lowest level of humanity. This general outline must obviously be carefully filled in for an accurate understanding.

An important first step is to study the social origins of officers and men. Also important is the fact that relationships among individuals in a military society are characteristically determined by hierarchical rank. We must determine, therefore, the extent to which the military hierarchy reflects the social hierarchy. And finally, the position of the army within society depends not only on the importance attached to arms but also on the popular image of the soldier and in turn his image of the ordinary civilian.

7

The Social Composition
of Armies

IT HAS for too long been repeated without any amplification that
soldiers were recruited from the lowest elements in the towns. In
order to understand the social composition of the armies more
completely we must look closely at the many details of recruiting
and regional distribution, as well as the relative proportions of·
townsmen and peasants.

RECRUITING FACTORS

We are beginning to have fairly extensive information for the
French army. Let us look at the differences between it and other
armies in recruiting activity. It must be remembered that soldiers
in the regular French troops came from two sources, voluntary
enlistees and militiamen incorporated into the regular units. The
distinction is clear enough, but it is less important than one might
think. First of all, the incorporation of large numbers of militiamen only took place in wartime, and the proportion of such
men in the army was steadily reduced during the eighteenth century. From a figure of 46 percent of the recruits during the War of
the Spanish Succession, when all militiamen were incorporated,
it fell to 36 percent during the War of the Polish Succession (a

little less than one out of three militiamen called up); it was 30 percent during the War of the Austrian Succession (a little below one out of two), and 20 percent during the Seven Years War (less than one out of four). All the surviving militiamen who were called up were returned home after the wars except those who chose to remain with their regiments and enlisted for that purpose. And it should be added that the militiamen who expressed willingness to be sent into the regiments were the first to be called. Such cases were not unusual, for many of the men in the militia battalions were not there purely by chance; often they were men who in spite of regulations had been "bought" by their communities, that is they were volunteers; sometimes they were former soldiers (although the latter usually preferred to return directly to the army rather than proceed through a militia battalion).

Factors operating against recruitment are easily recognized. First of all, there was the conflict with other obligations—for example, in coastal areas, where in order that naval recruiting might be kept up the inhabitants were not allowed to enlist in the army. There were, of course, other vocations to attract men away from military service. Married men and those who had any hopes of inheriting an estate or rights to succession seldom enlisted. And finally the diminishing popular esteem for arms made recruiting increasingly difficult as the eighteenth century progressed.

In considering the traditional views on recruiting, we will look first at the least admirable motivations for enlistment. There is no question that the army appeared to be a refuge for any who wished to avoid all kinds of bondage: sons rebelling against parental authority or running away from punishment, fleeing family control; young men made impatient by social controls, the bonds of the parish or district or village community; those unwilling to work and thus avoiding judicial control, delinquents sometimes encouraged by authorities to enlist, men threatened by lawsuits, and others using the enlistment bonus to pay serious debts. There was also another category of men who joined to escape legal restraints: Protestants who found relative tolerance for their beliefs among the troops, who were generally unconcerned about religion.

Enlistment was also a means of escaping from miserable poverty, and recruiting was easiest in times of scarcity and famine. The records of enlistment bonuses provide a true indicator in this respect: In 1693–1694 and in 1710 men enlisted without even asking for the bonus (the *argent du roi*). They simply hoped to survive by enlisting. While varying according to particular conditions, bonuses continued to increase after 1715. Very important during wars, they were only slightly reduced when peace returned. The maximum of sixty livres, of which thirty livres was paid on enlistment and the rest on arrival and registration, was generally exceeded; during the Seven Years War the sum reached 500 livres for men of large physical stature. In all countries it was easier to obtain recruits for the cavalry and the dragoons than for the infantry; the former offered not only a certain prestige but superior wages and rations as well.

Psychological misery became an increasingly important factor. Widowers, orphans, uprooted foreign vagrants, especially men from the countryside who had not succeeded in finding positions in the cities looked to the army for human contact and support, perhaps following a comrade into service. The number of orphans among the enlisted men rose in the eighteenth century, probably because the distress of such people was revealed as more acute than had been acknowledged, as increasing attention was given to children in society. Often remarriage of the father had the same effect, and one may suppose that in some cases such enlistments were given hearty support.

Example was unquestionably important. The presence of troops stimulated many young men to join the colors, and recruitment was relatively successful in frontier provinces and garrison towns. It was not necessarily easier to carry out, however: recruiters, who knew who was available in these areas and did not have to search far from their units, were competing with one another. Moreover, the inhabitants, familiar with the ways of the army, knew how to protect themselves from the traps set by recruiters. Routes regularly used in troop movements played the same role as garrison centers, and as we might expect it was the isolated, poor regions away from the major highways that provided the fewest enlistees.

The force of example often acted very quickly, while a military "vocation" came about more slowly. Sometimes the latter simply reflected a turbulent or brutal nature or an adventurous spirit, and it was occasionally influenced by example as well. It is difficult to determine how much is due to example, however, in an attraction to a military calling. The spectacle of a parade, an overheard conversation, childhood reading—all could stimulate a desire to become a soldier as soon as an opportunity arose. Vocations that grew out of a family background were among the most common and the most permanent.

Finally, there is no doubt that patriotism played a part. It very likely influenced many enlistees in the year 1709, as it unquestionably did in 1792. But as Frenchmen seldom had occasion to defend their land or their political and cultural identities against foreign invasion during the course of the eighteeenth century, patriotism did not cause spectacular surges of enlistments. It is to be noted, however, that it made enlistment in foreign armies less frequent.

The factors just considered are general enough to be true on the whole for other armies. Certain adjustments must be made, however. We must remember that in Prussia the *Kantonsystem* meant a kind of permanent conscription after 1733, which supplemented voluntary enlistment. The Kantonists represented only 60 percent of the recruits under Frederick William I, and generally 50 percent after that; such figures are extremely high, however, among the armies of western Europe. In Sweden and Russia conscription played an important part, but it is difficult to assess the real number of soldiers who were not enlistees, because of a prevailing inconsistency in designating recruits. In Austria, Spain, and Piedmont, militiamen were involved to various extents in recruitment for the army during wartime. In the English army, where the needs were slight, recruits were usually raised during wartime in the various theaters of operation, that is, outside the British Isles. During the War of the Spanish Succession, however, the "press" was used, although with little positive effect.

Special consideration must be given to recruiting in Switzerland. The factor of poverty, which was certainly evident in the sixteenth century and did not entirely disappear later, gave way to a sense of vocation, example, tradition, and governmental encouragement. Some regiments were pledged by cantons which had signed agreements with foreign rulers, so that the latter could in effect make use of regiments that had been recruited by local authorities. In other cases it was the colonel who negotiated and recruited, within the framework of arrangements made by the canton. Such recruiting was thus legal, and foreign service became a national industry and a source of revenue for the cantons. Individuals who enlisted on their own were less common, although they were to be found in cavalries. Swiss regiments appeared in nearly all European armies: Savoy-Piedmont (1480–1832), France (1496–1830), Austria (1498 to the end of the eighteenth century), Venice (1511–1719),the Church States (1506–1870), Spain (1515–1823), Genoa (1573–1779), England (1690–1856), Holland (1676–1828), Prussia (1696–1848), Saxony (1704–1814), Naples (1731–1859). There were up to 30,000 Swiss in foreign service at one time. Their loyalty was such that rulers had no hesitation in introducing Swiss units into their guards, units like the *Cent-Suisses* of France, Prussia, Piedmont, Lorraine, and, for a short time, Austria. One could say, paradoxically, that service abroad was a way for the Swiss to express their national spirit. Swiss regiments everywhere formed first of all an army within an army, having their own special codes and forms of justice. Eventually an international rule arose that Swiss regiments were not to be made to fight against one another.

Hussar mercenaries were another matter. After the victorious counteroffensives of the Imperial troops against the Turks, the western armies became aware of the value of light cavalry, and hussar regiments were formed of men from diverse backgrounds, often adventurers from the Danube and Balkan regions. They retained their ethnic character until around 1725, preferring to change armies rather than weapons.

Recruiting of a patriotic nature took place in invaded countries, especially when they had been plundered: the United Provinces (1672), Upper Austria (1683), Russia (1709), Sweden (1719), Poland, at the appeal of Kosciusko (1794). And again, recruiting foreigners, except for the Swiss, became increasingly difficult in the eighteenth century, particularly from different language regions. France had to fill up her German regiments with men from Alsace and Lorraine, and French prisoners of war signed up by Frederick II deserted en masse. Generally speaking, the reduction in popular esteem for the military profession did not bring about a comparable reduction in psychological motivations for recruitment.

REGIONAL COMPOSITION

A regional assessment of recruiting would in theory have meaning only for voluntary armies. For militias or for armies using a canton system or conscription, such an analysis would seem to be inappropriate, since each English county, each French district, each Swedish or Prussian canton, or each group of 100,000 Russians, had to furnish a specified number of recruits. In fact, however, voluntary enlistment took place in all armies, and the other recruiting methods simply provided the numbers needed to make up the required total. Moreover, the determination of quotas for each regional or numerical group often took into account the degree of difficulty encountered in recruiting. We can at times, with caution, include in our study the regional distribution of insubordination and desertion, as these factors acted as a counterpart to the attractions of a military career. Finally, we must note that regional or even ethnic units were an important element in central and eastern Europe.

Here again the French example can serve as a point of departure, as it is possible to make systematic use of the troop registers of the ancien regime. Without using such sources it is nearly impossible to attempt these regional investigations for the sixteenth and seventeenth centuries. We observe first of all that recruiting may often present a regional character that is in no way institutional or official, and that the names of provinces that are given to many regiments are not accurate. The Auvergne Regiment was mostly recruited in the Cévennes and in Protestant areas. In the early eighteenth century the Vivarais Regiment was recruited in the Perche and upper Maine districts before shifting its base to southern Languedoc. This is explained by the fact that such a unit included captains and colonels from a single province, and that these officers preferred to seek recruits in their own districts or even on their own estates. To add to this, the incorporation of men from militia battalions into such regional regiments during wartime temporarily swelled the proportion of men native to the region that had originally supplied the battalion.

It is possible to map recruitment areas, in spite of the great number of soldiers and the unevenness of the sources. It is more difficult to relate them to the populations of the different districts, as figures for the latter are unreliable. A comparison of maps showing the regional composition of the army in 1716, 1763, and 1789 reveals certain constants as well as an evolution. The provinces of the south and west provided proportionally fewer recruits than those of the north and east: more than 1,200 soldiers for every 10,000 citizens in the Evêchés [the bishoprics of Metz, Toul, and Verdun], Lorraine, and Franche-Comté in 1789; less than 150 per 10,000 in Brittany and La Rochelle; and less than 350 per 10,000 in the districts of Tours, Orléans, Bourges, Moulins, Riom, Limoges, Poitiers, Bordeaux, Auch, and Pau. Proximity to the frontier had one effect, the sea had the opposite. The height of the natives (theoretically, a foot soldier had to be 5 feet 2 inches, a cavalier or grenadier, 5 feet 4 inches) was probably a considerable factor in the geographical variation in recruitment. The cavalry and the artillery were more extensively recruited in the north than was the infantry, although that region did not particularly correspond to the areas where horses were most frequently raised or used. Also operating was the factor of the "disposition," or "capability" of the people, reflected to some extent in their level of prosperity. It is not surprising that the relatively rich areas like the Loire, for example, rejected military service except when special emergencies arose. And we find that the militiamen who most readily agreed to remain in the corps were often from poor districts. We should observe that northern Normandy constituted an exception in the western and coastal areas after the middle of the century, in the fairly large number of recruits that it supplied. In effect, the threat of English invasion turned Normandy into a frontier province.

Changes in recruiting patterns during the eighteenth century show further concentration toward the northern and eastern provinces. The number of men native to the districts of Brittany, Tours, Orléans, La Rochelle, Bordeaux, Auch, Pau, Bourges, Limoges, Moulins, and Riom shrank, while men from Amiens, Châlons, Alsace, Besançon, and Caen appeared in greater numbers. Recruiting for the artillery was concentrated in areas where artillery units were stationed: Soissons, Metz, Nancy, Besançon, Alsace. This evolution reveals that recently annexed frontier regions quickly took on the role of eastern defensive border areas for the kingdom.

A study of desertions sheds little light for an understanding of regional military vocation in the case of France. Frontier regions (Flanders and the Pyrenees), seacoast districts, and apparently those areas from which emigration was common were the sources of the most deserters; but it does not follow—except for coastal districts—that their military vocation was less. It is difficult to assess recruiting in terms of quality, but we can approach the task by considering the regional origins of the grenadiers (soldiers of outstanding height, but also in principle elite troops) and company officers. Recruitment maps confirm the readiness to join up in the northern and eastern provinces and reveal that if recruiting in the southern provinces was low in quantity, it was generally high in quality. Pau was the district that supplied the most subaltern officers in relation to the total number of recruits. The origins of the subalterns often reflected the poverty of these men, who had either risen from the ranks or were too poor to purchase a company. It was the poorest districts that supplied the greatest number of such officers.

The number of city-bred or country-bred soldiers appears at first glance easy to determine, but we cannot tell whether some of those originally from the country had left their homes and attempted to establish themselves in the towns before joining the army. Close to two out of three recruits were born in the country, less than the proportion of the rural population in the kingdom as a whole but many more than we are led to expect by contemporary statements. Probably a considerable number were products of the rural exodus; this appears to be indicated by the higher age of recruits born in the country. Whatever the reason, the overall proportion of those of rural origin rose slightly from 62 percent in 1716 to 67 percent in 1763; but for native Frenchmen it rose only from 62 percent to 65 percent. (This lesser increase for French-born soldiers may be accounted for by the fact that the incorporation of militiamen, primarily of rural origin, was much less frequent during the Seven Years War than in preceding years.)

The increase reflects the growing reluctance of city dwellers to serve in the armies; their attitude explains why the system of incorporating militias was not used in French towns until after 1743 and why in Paris itself lot-drawing was rejected after 1744. It is quite possible that the idea of military service was less frightening to country dwellers, especially those from frontier areas. Obviously city dwellers did not behave in the same way everywhere: garrison towns and towns with large industries provided more soldiers than towns whose primary role was religious, parliamentary, academic, or administrative.

It is hard to say whether recruits from towns were better than those from the country. The latter provided more grenadiers, corporals, and cavalry brigadiers, that is, strong and loyal soldiers without special talents; and country men generally stayed in their units longer than city men. On the other hand, the countryside provided fewer noncommissioned officers, sergeants, and quartermaster sergeants, that is, men who could read and write and otherwise assume responsibility.

The only region for which we have studies comparable in detail to those that have been done in France is the Netherlands, where recruiting of national regiments has been investigated by Joseph Ruwet. As in France, fairly clear differences were found from one province to another, from 91 recruits for every 10,000 inhabitants in Luxembourg to 15 for every 10,000 in Guelders. The effect of foreign recruiting can only partly explain these differences; regions linguistically related to neighboring countries, although combed by foreign recruiters, were still major sources for soldiers. The Low Germans (close to 100 recruits for every 10,000 inhabitants) and the Walloons (between 42 and 86 per 10,000) served more readily than the Flemings (from 36 to 41 per 10,000). This variation in interest appears again in the distribution of deserters. Flanders, with 35.2 percent of the population, provided 26.2 percent of the recruits and 38.5 percent of the deserters. It seems clear that in addition to the cultural affinities that favorably affected recruiting in the areas linguistically related to Germany and France, the "disposition" of the citizens produced the same effects as in France. Areas of major economic activity furnished fewer recruits than others (Guelders was a special case). Additionally, in areas with high recruitment, like Luxembourg and Limburg, enlistment generally took place at a lower age. And we find again that the regions with the highest recruitment success were those from which the most emigration took place.

The distribution of city dwellers and country dwellers also reveals the traits and the evolution we found for France. Urban recruitment fell in the Ninth Infantry Regiment from three men out of four in the middle of the century to 54 percent in 1787. The increase in the number on active duty furnishes a partial explanation: recruiting in the towns would have reached a saturation point in the middle of the century, but countrymen could fill in for them after that. What was found to be true for France concerning the greater or lesser recruitment success according to the kind of activity characterizing a particular town also holds true for the Austrian Netherlands.

For other countries we must be content, while awaiting the results of current investigations, with very general statements left for us by contemporary officers. To these we can add evidence on foreign soldiers in the French army who had served in their own national armies. To the extent that we can draw conclusions from incomplete information, it appears that city dwellers outnumbered countrymen, except in the cases of soldiers from central or eastern Europe or those secured by contracts between the French king and Swiss cantons or independent princes.

Probably as a response to claims that it was difficult to recruit in certain provinces, as much as because of proximity to the frontier, the Spanish provinces were unevenly affected by militia call-ups. We remember that in 1692 the province of Zamora, without its city, had to furnish 22 men out of 100 on its list of militiamen, while Valladolid was only required to send 6. The capital cities of these two provinces only owed 15 and 4.5 percent, respectively, possibly because they were already supplying more volunteers.

We know that the western provinces of the Prussian kingdom were not bound by the *Kantonsystem*; they do not seem to have produced as many soldiers as the provinces of Brandenburg, Prussia, and Pomerania. It is still impossible to acquire an exact understanding of the relative success and importance of recruiting in the diverse countries of the Austrian monarchy. It does not appear that raising men was very difficult in the military districts. With no large cities, recruiting largely yielded peasants; it was often closely linked to colonization. The same is true for the Russian monarchy. Although the *Indelningsverket* superficially evened out recruiting in most of Sweden, it seems that the attitudes of the inhabitants toward military service varied from one place to another. In 1719 citizens in the Stockholm region responded fairly well to special levies, but men in areas farther from the capital frequently ran off to the woods to avoid serving. At the time, it is true, the capital was under threat of a Russian invasion.

It is probable that certain general factors found in France and the Austrian Netherlands were operating elsewhere, although many others certainly intervened in each country. In general, recruits seem to have come more often from towns than from villages, but it is not certain that in all countries men from urban backgrounds were more numerous than country men. The many forms of compulsory service had the common goal of drawing strong peasants, who were not very eager to volunteer for the army, away from the countryside. Moreover, in the interests of developing industries in their countries, the eastern rulers protected artisans from the recruiters, even going so far as to guarantee exemption to any foreign craftsmen whom they could attract. This attitude is probably one explanation for the fact that in the eighteenth century the different forms of compulsory service were practiced most extensively in the predominantly rural countries like Sweden, Russia, and also Prussia.

We can, then, in analyzing the geographical origins of the soldiers, perceive two general categories: on the one hand are found the armies of the eastern and northern countries, in which despite the reluctance of peasants to leave their farms the proportion of rural soldiers is large, as the distribution of the inhabitants would suggest; and on the other hand we have the armies of the west—France, the Netherlands, Spain, Piedmont, England—where recruits were at first produced primarily by the towns, but where the proportion of country-born increased slowly for a number of reasons: the general rural exodus, the calling-up of militiamen, and the growing familiarity with the idea of military service (although most were still opposed to it).

SOCIAL COMPOSITION

It is even more difficult to assess social composition accurately than to define regional composition. To my knowledge no general study has been published for countries other than France and the Austrian Netherlands. We can approach the task using traditional methods, but any quantitative inquiry must rely on registers, which are difficult to use and often deceptive in terms of statistics. Registers were supposed to list the status of each soldier and of his father—in effect, their professions. Only a few officers, however, carried out the task of enrollment thoroughly. Even if we assume that recruits gave accurate information about themselves and their families, registering officers often set it down or interpreted it in such a way that all their descriptions would be consistent. These practices increased the confusion caused by language differences (due to dialects and technical language) or variations in social patterns from one province to another. There is a danger, if we are not careful, of adding together wealthy farmer-cultivators of the north of France and farmhands of other provinces; or "bourgeois," referring to those listed on the town (or "burg") registers, and "bourgeois," meaning

the middle classes, in the modern sense of the word. An indication of trade followed does not always give the position occupied
within it—master, journeyman, or apprentice. Dual trades were
ignored, and the note, *"sans vacation"* [no profession], or the
absence of any information about a recruit's status could mean
either that he lived on income from an estate or that he had no
regular position. Very likely an examination of social composition
in other armies will encounter the same difficulties.

We can state for one thing that the number of soldiers' sons
among recruits was low, on the order of two percent; most were
"enfants du corps," that is, born within the regiment, usually the
sons of lower officers and in a sense "adopted" by the unit. Such a
low percentage is not surprising, considering that marriage by
soldiers was disapproved of in France (in contrast to the attitude
in the armies of central Europe) and also that few of these children reached the age of sixteen.

Given the low esteem among gentlemen and wealthy citizens
for service in the ranks, soldiers with these social backgrounds
can be considered as déclassés. But we cannot know if such dis-
placement was caused by their enlistment or by some decline that
had begun earlier. There seems to be little doubt that poverty was
one reason for a gentleman to enlist, if he could neither keep up
appearances as a cadet nor purchase a company. The proportion
of gentlemen is difficult to estimate, since after the middle of the
eighteenth century many concealed their aristocratic origins,
only acknowledging them in order to obtain dismissal more easily. The percentage of gentlemen among the troops may well
have been greater than the proportion of nobles within the nation
as a whole. They were found more often in the cavalry than in
the infantry.

The proportion of commoners that we can classify as sons of
"notables" (for example, non-military officers, solid citizens, professional men, businessmen, manufacturers) was seven percent
in 1716 and four percent in 1763. If we attempt to set apart a kind
of elite among the ordinary people—a "popular elite"—by

somewhat arbitrarily grouping clerks, master craftsmen and journeymen of trades classified as "arts," and merchants (or independent farmers and millers in rural districts) we find about 10 percent with such backgrounds; this figure became lower as the century progressed.

In contrast, sons of craftsmen below the level of master rose from 34 percent to 40 percent between 1716 and 1763. Among these, rural artisans were slightly greater in number than urban artisans. Farmworkers (because of the great number listed under this category we cannot consider them among the well-off farmers, except in Flanders, Artois, Picardy, upper Normandy, and the regions just north of Paris), winegrowers, and small gardeners went from 36 percent to 40 percent in the same period. The number of city and rural day-laborers, on the other hand, doubled, from 7 percent to 14 percent. We note that men of the upper categories, as well as the farmworkers, preferred to enlist in the cavalry although advancement was slower, while the sons of soldiers, artisans, and laborers more often joined the infantry.

Generalized as these estimates are, it appears to be true that recruitment in the higher social categories, including the popular elite, followed a downward trend during the eighteenth century. This was true for the sons of farmworkers as well. In contrast, the proportion of sons of artisans and laborers became greater. Does this evolution mean there were two opposing attitudes in regard to military service? Of course the army of 1716 was what remained of the large army of the War of the Spanish Succession, an army that had called out many bourgeois and farmers' sons who would not otherwise have joined up but who were able to adapt to military life. The wars of Louis XV did not have the same result. Throughout the century, service in the ranks was gradually left to more humble social groups. The withdrawal was particularly evident among the sons of "notables" between 1716 and 1737, and among those of the popular elite between 1737 and 1763.

The gradual movement toward artisans is still more clearly

seen if we consider the positions of the fathers of the recruits. In most cases where a soldier's profession differed from his father's, the change was away from an agricultural profession toward some kind of handicraft trade.

The ages of the recruits varied according to social position. Setting aside the sons of military men, it was the sons of gentlemen and bourgeois at one extreme, and of laborers at the other, who were the youngest enlistees. Enlistment of older men was more frequent during wars than in peacetime.

The educational level of the soldiers, if we go by what is indicated by the signatures in marriage records, appears to have been lower than that of the popular classes as a whole (see Chapter 9).

Access to higher ranks was affected by social origins. Although most noncommissioned officers were voluntary enlistees, there were militiamen among them as well. Gentlemen, bourgeois, and men of the popular elite, as well as sons of soldiers, were more often noncommissioned officers than were the sons of artisans, farmworkers, or day-laborers; this situation became more pronounced as the century progressed.

A comparison of the positions of the recruits with those of their fathers gives an impression of great social stability, though we must remember that many young recruits had not yet reached an age to be professionally established. There were also some instances of social mobility, particularly among those who became subordinate officers. Sometimes it was an upward movement, for example, for a recruit who had learned a trade that could be called an "art," while his father practiced a humbler trade; or a recruit who claimed a trade but called his father a day-laborer. In such a case achieving the rank of sergeant could perhaps be looked upon as a confirmation of his rise. More frequently, any social mobility that took place before enlistment was a downward one.

The social distribution of soldiers according to their regional origins does not appear to reflect precisely the social structures of individual provinces. The provinces that provided the most soldiers from the upper social groups were fairly often those in which recruiting activity was weakest, and also those which furnished the most subordinate officers. The eastern provinces were among those characterized by recruitment primarily from the lower classes.

We cannot give statistical evidence for any other armies except the regiments of the Austrian Netherlands studied by Ruwet. Registers for foreign corps in the French army reveal very little about social origins, except for the Swiss; sons of military men are relatively numerous among Swiss troops. It is impossible to know how many men of rural origins followed agricultural trades, because only handicraft trades are mentioned. As for foreign soldiers in French units, full information is available only for men of French background but from areas not directly under the rule of the French king (Lorraine, Savoy, Franche-Comté); such information conforms to what has been said about the king's subjects. The registers for the national regiments of the Netherlands give little indication of status other than craft trades. As in France, the military trades were well represented, particularly those of cobbler and tailor; such skills were, of course, routinely reported, and it is also possible that some recruits, hoping to raise the price for their enlistment, may have claimed them falsely. It is likely that those who had learned these trades hoped to be able to use them in the army. Again, the proportion of recruits who had been living by agriculture seems to have shrunk, as the proportion of artisans rose.

It appears, in the absence of other studies, that the social composition of the other western armies was in many ways like that of the French army and the national regiments of the Austrian Netherlands. This seems to be clearly the case in Spain, Piedmont, Bavaria, Austria, and the United Provinces. Despite the periodic addition of militiamen to the troops in Spain, Piedmont, and Bavaria, peasants appear to have been fewer than artisans. In

England, according to contemporary writers, recruitment was carried out only at the lowest social level and among social outcasts. On the other hand, in Sweden, Russia, and Prussia, for reasons already indicated, the number of peasants was very large. And we can add that in the Swedish, Prussian, and Austrian armies the number of married men was greater than the 15 percent in the French troops, and the number of soldiers' sons was much higher; the opposite may be true for the number of gentlemen serving in the ranks.

In general terms, it appears that wherever recruiting was regionally organized and based on militias, canton systems, or military districts, recruits for positions as subordinate officers were likely to be produced from the popular elite as well as from military families. This finding is particularly valid for militias, in which the military hierarchy most naturally mirrored the local social hierarchy.

8

Military and Social
Hierarchies

WE HAVE ALREADY referred to a rivalry between the nobility and
the bourgeoisie for positions as officers. This rivalry was often
manifested as a simple contest between birth on the one hand
and skill, or more often money, on the other. It affected not only
promotion but the training of future officers as well. We have
seen, too, that the nobility fairly willingly left the officers' positions in the technical corps—engineers and artillery—to men of
bourgeois origins. These general outlines are too simple, however. Connections with the ruler or the court, the presence of
aristocrats of different ethnic groups in the same unit, service
abroad—all these must be taken into consideration. Furthermore, historians have usually limited their studies to the recruiting and promotion of officers, whereas similar social rivalries
were found among noncommissioned officers; men from the
middle classes, the popular elite, and even the lesser nobility,
competed for positions as sergeants, just as noblemen competed
with bourgeois for lieutenants' places. In looking at these problems, which arose in all of the European armies, it is appropriate
to examine the hierarchy of offices in the different armies, and to
review some general observations concerning the factors affecting promotion.

THE MILITARY HIERARCHY AND PROMOTION

The military hierarchies in all the armies of Europe were for all practical purposes fixed by the beginning of the eighteenth century. As military organization tended to become similar from one country to another, we find that the various command classifications became nearly uniform, too; often the same names were used, having been taken for the most part from Latin. Such uniformity was due to Italian and Spanish influence spread by the Renaissance in the sixteenth century, and later to the influence of military innovations in France under Louis XIV. It was sometimes only superficial, however, for in most armies the same designation could apply to a title, an office, a function, or a rank. Moreover the selling of the positions of colonel and captain became standard in some armies (among them the English and the French), and in France the practice of inheriting these positions became widespread, more or less unofficially, particularly in the foreign regiments. Thus a certain prestigious regiment might "belong" to a proprietary colonel of high birth, perhaps the sovereign himself but usually a prince—sometimes foreign—who did not actually command it but who nevertheless took part in the appointing of officers. In such a case the title of "colonel" was in practical terms comparable to a title of nobility. The regiment was, then, commanded by a *colonel lieutenant* or *colonel commandant*, or in the absence of such a grade it might be led by an officer of lieutenant-colonel grade, temporarily carrying out the functions of colonel. In France at the end of the eighteenth century there was a rise in the number of *colonels en second*, officers who had the grade of colonel but did not regularly carry out a colonel's duties.

It was the same, at least in the French army, at the company level, where there were both proprietary captains and lieutenant captains. There were also captains of the foot, with both the grade and the functions of captain, as well as numerous *capitaines à la suite* and *capitaines réformés*. The latter were officers whose companies had been reorganized or at least partially demobilized during peacetime but who nevertheless retained their grade. In the French army a sizable group of these second-level captains arose, men who had no command or who acted as lieutenants; there were so many that the practice developed of giving the grade of *capitaine réformé* to lieutenants, who "owned" no companies. At the end of the eighteenth century, it became standard practice for a *capitaine en second* to serve alongside a commanding captain.

We should observe, too, that in the units constituting the royal guards, all officers held a grade higher than the functions they carried out. In the French guards regiment all captains held the title of colonel, and lieutenants held the title of lieutenant colonel, or even higher.

For officers carrying out administrative duties, the classification of "*commissaire*," widespread throughout Europe, covered even greater diversity, and a qualitative "hierarchy" was set up: regional, provincial, or ordinary commissaries. On the whole, the organization of army staffs, although based on certain key positions, took many different forms.

All of these classifications caused confusion when prisoner exchanges took place. Exchange arrangements led to the laborious and often disputed establishment of corresponding "values" for classifications used in the different armies. We can see how difficult it must have been to verify "career lines" within an army and to compare these lines from one army to another.

Advancement to officer level took on even greater importance when matters other than purely military activity were concerned. Even in armies based on voluntary enlistment, the potential or aptitude for "producing men" was no longer the essential criterion for advancement. As the State extended its authority over the army it gradually set the rules for promotion. An aptitude for command was an often-mentioned ideal criterion. In the six-teenth century moral strength and heroism were called for; in the eighteenth century, when military training became more impor-tant, talent was more often sought after. The social order of the ancien regime favored the nobility in promotion to officer posi-tions, but, as we have seen, money still counted, even for access to non-salable positions. With the rise of permanent armies and the increasing professionalism of the officers, more importance was accorded to merit; but, as "exceptional service" by definition was uncommon, "merit" tended to mean "seniority," either in years of service or in office or responsibility.

There were of course other factors, less measurable and less dependable. First of all, there was favoritism, acknowledged as a part of a society based on "connections" but becoming less open in the eighteenth century, except in the choice of the highest level of commanding officer. And we must count the element of luck. The *officier de fortune* was not a rich man but one who had risen from the ranks and who had had the good luck to remain alive and to be able to distinguish himself. Even in an age when life expectancy was low, a military career was looked upon as an elimination game; only those lucky enough to survive could be promoted.

These factors—birth, wealth, talent, merit, favor, luck—were not mutually exclusive. We observe that luck, although not exactly a social factor, favored those with wealth, who did not have to remain subordinate officers or wait for their epaulettes through long years of combat and epidemics. Heavy tolls were taken of the junior officers, especially those who because of high birth had become officers at an age characterized by more brav-ery than experience. Mortality was probably even higher among the men, however, than among the officers, because of epidem-ics, particularly in winter quarters. It must be remembered that even in peacetime the average life-span in the eighteenth century was still only half or even one-third that of today.

This brief review of the factors affecting advancement would be incomplete without consideration of the military rewards used by Louis XIV to acknowledge merit without granting promotion. Orders of knighthood had both a military and an aristocratic value. After the sixteenth century the first element gradually gave way to the second, and after attempting in 1671 to transform the Order of Saint Lazare and the Order of Mount Carmel into pensions for old officers, Louis XIV in 1693 created the Order of Saint Louis with separate grades: chevaliers, officers, commanders; it was expanded in 1759 by the Order of Military Merit, intended for foreign Protestant officers. The Order of Saint Louis was copied abroad, by the Order of the Sword in Sweden (1748), by the Order of Saint George in Russia (1769), or by military sections of orders also conferred upon civilians (like the Prussian Order of Merit, which eventually became entirely military in 1810). The French practice also led to the adaptation of older orders for the purpose of military recompense: the Order of the Danebrog in Denmark, the orders of Saint Maurice and Saint Lazarus in Piedmont. The French Order of Saint Louis was eventually used particularly to recognize seniority in the service, and in 1781 an *ordonnance* specified that to receive the cross without having performed some outstanding service it was necessary to have spent eighteen consecutive years as a colonel, twenty-four as a lieutenant colonel, twenty-six as a captain, or twenty-eight as a lieutenant, second lieutenant, or ensign. Years of service in the ranks were counted, for officers, as one year for every two actually spent, while years on active campaign duty counted double. Noncommissioned officers and soldiers could only acquire the cross for outstanding actions.

The granting of pensions, honors, and decorations meant that the element of merit in actual promotion was supplanted by other factors. And it ensured the persistence of certain mental attitudes, including the assumption that general officers' positions should be assigned to the higher nobility, field officers' or company officers' places to the lower nobility, and company officers' posts, at best, to the middle classes. These attitudes undoubtedly conflicted with efforts to assign responsibilities to capable men only, and with the ambitions of the social groups least favored in the distribution of commissions. Attitudes and assumptions like these aroused animosity, particularly at those levels, like lieutenant or lieutenant colonel, that could represent a final career goal for some or a step along the way upward for others.

We will now see if the reality in the principal armies of Europe corresponded to this general outline. A social and moral crisis took place in the French army in the late eighteenth century, while the armies of the other countries—although possessing similar administrative structures—did not undergo similar major upheavals. The French situation will be considered separately.

COUNTRIES WITH CONVENTIONAL
PROMOTION POLICIES

The countries in which the military hierarchy conformed fairly closely to the social hierarchy can be divided into three categories: for most of the countries of continental Europe the general outline sketched above can be applied with almost no exceptions; noble status was the principal criterion in the recruitment of officers, but merit entered in, to some extent, in advancement. In England, the principal factor affecting promotion was wealth. And in the Mediterranean countries the nobility as a whole was so lacking in military ambition that social problems in the army were less acute than in other countries.

The profession of military officer lost prestige in Italy after the early sixteenth century, and a similar change took place in Spain a century later. Aristocrats, often living in cities, found army life less attractive. In Italy, with the exception of Piedmont and the kingdom of Naples, those with military interests turned to the Hapsburg or Bourbon armies. Even after princes of these two houses were installed in Tuscany and Parma, the central Italian states maintained only enough troops to keep order, and the army of Naples offered little to attract the impoverished nobles of that kingdom. In Spain, once the War of Succession was over (1714), the grandees preferred to stay at court, where arms had only a decorative or ceremonial function. The many hidalgos were drawn to administrative positions, although it has been said that "they did not scorn arms, but scorned armies." Philip V opened the lower ranks to middle-class young men who were living in the style of gentlemen, and when Charles III reduced the number of officers in order to save money there was less objection than there might have been elsewhere.

In the other continental states, maintenance of an army that grew steadily larger (except in Sweden) led sovereigns to exert some pressure when interest on the part of the nobility in military careers was not great enough to fill all the officer posts; this was particularly true in Piedmont. Opening the lower grades to commoners led to friction everywhere, except in the technical branches, but it remained fairly easy to earn a title by carrying out military responsibilities.

It was in Prussia that the nobility were—by the ruler's desire—most closely tied to the army. At the time of the Great Elector, officers with common backgrounds could still rise to high positions; records show that three were the sons of peasants. In 1704 Frederick I again guaranteed that commoners would have equal chances for promotion with noblemen, and the granting of titles was at that time fairly common. But Frederick William I changed these arrangements, and the reorganization of the troops in 1713 was fatal for many commoners. In 1739 no more than 11 out of 211 staff officers came from lower-class backgrounds. On the other hand, commoners made up half of the engineers corps and appeared in large numbers among the hussars. Frederick II continued his predecessor's policy, except during the Seven Years War; in 1786 only 10 percent of the officers were commoners, and most of these were kept apart in garrison battalions or in the artillery; there were only 22 among the 689 staff officers. Just before the Battle of Jena, the Prussian army included only 695 commoners out of 7,000 to 8,000 officers: 289 in artillery, 83 in the three garrison battalions, 82 on sick leave, 84 in the cavalry, especially in the hussars, 131 in the infantry (75 in the light infantry), and about 30 staff officers.

Admittedly, Frederick II granted titles of nobility for military service fairly readily. He decided in 1768 that after ten years of service as garrison or artillery captain a commoner could be ennobled. In these corps, too, middle-class noncommissioned officers could become company officers fairly easily. On the other hand, Frederick II made an effort to do away with the granting of titles for money.

As long as Frederick II lived, this advancement system led to no serious social conflicts. The royal authority alone does not account for this. In the absence of a powerful court society the land-based nobility formed a somewhat homogeneous unit. And on the other hand, the *Kompaniewirtschaft* insured that all those who moved fairly rapidly up to captain grade had equal opportunities for further advancement. Finally, the rigorous nature of army service and the few chances of rising to superior officer positions discouraged the relatively few middle-class military men from seeking social promotion through corps other than the artillery and the engineers. The *Kantonsystem* easily supplied enough noncommissioned officers.

We find more officers of peasant or commoner backgrounds in the other German states. In Saxony, in 1808, there were 347 out of 1,210, some 29 percent. In the Bavarian army, high posts went to noblemen (often foreigners), and among the company officers were many men risen from the ranks and volunteers who were officers' sons. (There was a tendency for noblemen and officers' sons to mix.) In the cadet corps that had been formed in 1756 in imitation of Prussia, there were, in 1791, 84 commoners and 34 noblemen or men who had been granted titles. In the Württemberg army the proportion of commoners was lower. According to a ruling of 1754 a noncommissioned officer could become a second lieutenant after three years of service if he had a title, and after twelve years if he was from the lower classes.

At the end of the seventeenth century, many officers in the Austrian army were either from the German lesser nobility or of central European origins; most lacked wealth or property, or were the younger sons of great families, according to Barker. Advancement was evidently rapid, up to 1718, as a large army was being organized and wars were continually being waged against France and the Ottoman Empire. During the decade from 1730 to 1740 the number of officers recruited from among both foreigners and commoners decreased, and the rate of promotion slowed down. Under Maria Theresa the army again became generally accessible for commoners, but they remained restricted to the company-officer grades. The case of Kléber is illustrative: having studied mathmatics and architecture in Paris and then attended the military academy in Munich, Kléber enlisted in the Kaunitz regiment in 1776 and reached the level of lieutenant. He returned to France in 1783, declaring that advancement was nearly impossible for commoners. Equality of opportunity even among aristocrats was more limited in the Austrian army than in the Prussian army, for the court played a greater role; extreme discrimination and resentment were usually avoided, however, as merit was a fairly influential element in selection, from the reign of Maria Theresa on.

In Russia officer posts became in principle a monopoly of the nobility. Peter the Great had required aristocrats to serve. In 1742 their terms were limited to twenty-four years, but in fact some boyars enrolled their sons in a guards regiment while they were still in the cradle, thus enabling them to be free of obligation when about twenty-five. In 1762 Peter III allowed nobles to retire from service whenever they wished. The sons of landowners, particularly aristocrats, could begin their service in St. Petersburg in one of the elite regiments, or after 1730 in the corps of noble cadets. The military school for cadets was formed in 1766, and most officers who went on to outstanding careers passed through this academy. Court influence often opposed the element of merit in the assignment of higher commissions, and—particularly after the late eighteenth century—the sons of Russian aristocrats were often appointed at a very tender age.

In Sweden the overlap between noble and lower-class officers took place at the regimental level, as officers had to have served previously as noncommissioned officers. Research in this field is now in progress, but in the meantime we can observe, along with Nordmann, certain trends in the social composition of the body of officers. While at the beginning of the wars of Charles XII (1700) 80 percent of the officers belonged to the old aristocracy, in 1718 we find 2,600 commoners and 1,300 nobles; and of the latter many were foreigners or had been granted titles only during recent campaigns. The *trabans*, or guards, provided another important route for social promotion. This extreme situation did not last long, however; lower-class officers were often the victims of reductions in the number of men in active duty, even under the *Indelningsverket*. In 1757 only 400 out of 1,400 officers were of common origin, most of them in the technical branches. In the infantry, newly created nobility could reach superior-officer level only with great difficulty, and in the cavalry, commoners hardly ever rose beyond cornet or ensign. The nobility were not necessarily at an advantage, however, since the sale and purchase of commissions was gradually introduced, with the device of the *accord*, which was similar to the *concordat* of the French officers. There were complaints about the influence of money in advancement, and in 1756 promotions "by choice" were suppressed; but the granting of titles continued to be common. Although Gustavus III would have preferred to have noble rather than commoner officers, the demands of his military policies—one of the purposes of which was, incidentally, to keep the nobles busy—increased the number of officers required. He had to turn to commoners, whose numbers went from 25 percent in 1780 to 34 percent in 1790. After the Anjala conspiracy (1788) he even replaced the noble officers of his guard with more reliable commoners.

In all these states men of humble birth could become officers, but they could not usually rise very far in the hierarchy. The absence of serious friction between nobles and commoners was largely due to the weakness of the middle class. Even in countries in which the court exerted a powerful influence, the situation was not the same as that in France. Competition for appointment to the highest positions was less extreme, as a captain's rank was less despised than in France, although the buying and selling of commissions affected relationships among officers everywhere.

The military and the social hierarchies were parallel in England also, but there they were based on a scale of wealth as much as birth. There are many reasons for this. First, as in the Mediterranean countries, many Englishmen were not interested in military careers. (This attitude did not prevail among the Scots, who filled a quarter of the officers' positions in the British army.) Next is the fact that the gentry and the bourgeoisie held fairly similar interests, and as the social hierarchy was based on wealth rather than birth the latter entered only in the sense of stimulating some initial interest. Thus most officers were younger sons of gentlemen. Those living on their estates preferred to serve in the militia, while non-resident gentry were more likely to join the regular army. The number of gentlemen serving in the army without commissions, as well as the number of commoners with commissions, decreased greatly during the eighteenth century; this tendency meant a clear separation of commissioned officers from noncommissioned officers, as the first were recruited from the gentry and the second, from commoners.

Within the gentry, wealth created distinctions. According to

Eric Robson, the English army was the only one in Europe in which the buying and selling of commissions was universally practiced: all positions became open to this kind of transfer, and in 1720 George I was forced to acknowledge the fact and set maximum fees. Such fees were particularly high within the old regiments that were kept active in peacetime. The purchase of a commission was looked on as a lifetime investment, and its sale provided income for a widow. Patronage influenced appointments, and the power of money was so great that wealth became a prerequisite for a military career, as "legal qualifications" were imposed on candidates. To apply for a commission they had to possess landed estates or be able to prove rights to an income with a value proportionate to the level of office sought. These requirements were imposed in the militias in 1757 and in the army in 1760. J. R. Western reported that in the militia of 1757 owners of estates had to control a revenue of at least £50 sterling to be an ensign, £100 to be a lieutenant, £200 to be a captain, £300 to be a major or a lieutenant colonel, and £400 to be a colonel. These sums were doubled for those who were only heirs to such property. Qualifications were less extreme for officers from Wales or from less prosperous counties like Cumberland or Westmorland. Between 1757 and 1802 costs rose for superior officers, but because of a shortage of candidates it was necessary to lower requirements for lieutenants and ensigns and to grant dispensations. After 1769, when the required income for an ensign was L20 and that for a colonel was L1,000, the gap continued to widen.

The career of a British officer, then, was determined from the beginning by the level of his wealth. Experience counted little in promotion. In fact, after the War of the League of Augsburg, older officers or those who became unnecessary upon the reduction of forces in peacetime received only half-pay. In spite of the small number of officer positions, the low prestige of the army assured a career to those who chose that profession, as long as

they had the necessary money. Although there was some improvement from the time of Pitt's ministry, only the artillery, like
the navy, escaped the tyranny of money.

SOCIAL CONFLICTS IN THE
FRENCH ARMY

In France recruiting problems and the promotion of officers
were apparently no different from those in other countries up to
the time of Louis XIV. During his reign, however, the extreme
need for officers as the nobility were slaughtered in the many
campaigns raised doubts about the social arrangements, and in
the eighteenth century the army saw an increase in social rivalry,
which became very bitter at the end of the Seven Years War. On
the whole, birth retained the same importance as in other continental armies, yet the role of money grew, as in England.
Conflicts between these two elements were more frequent and
more dramatic than elsewhere, and they occurred at all levels,
setting in opposition court aristocrats and impoverished aristocrats, nobility and bourgeoisie, bourgeoise and popular elite.

The French army had always included large numbers of
officers of commoner background, but their positions within the
body of officers and their possibilities for promotion varied.
Sixteenth-century chroniclers like Montluc and Brantôme
praised the heroic deeds of men of low birth because they felt that
such actions revealed exceptional quality when carried out by
such men; they were willing to concede that courage made up for
the defect of low birth. The edict of 1534 that created provincial
legions granted to commoners the right to rise by degrees from
one office to the next, up to the level of lieutenant (Article 56). It
was apparently impossible to imagine promotion for such men
beyond that level, however, except in extremely rare cases. Leaders who rose from low origins were not accorded equal respect
everywhere, however; promotion was more difficult for them in

Piedmont than in Picardy, for example. In the sixteenth century such officers were usually classified as sons of farmworkers. Gentlemen did not yet, apparently, fear conflict with urban middle-class sons; they were more apt to mistrust implanting in peasants' sons military attitudes and skills that might threaten the seigniorial regime. A combination of noble status with outstanding qualities was the key to the highest positions, either through command assignments or through access to the royal household corps.

Commoners, usually middle-class burghers who were loyal to the king, became officers during the Wars of Religion, and from 1560 to 1614 the estates-general repeatedly considered complaints from the nobility about this subject. The commons, or third estate, incidentally, did not insist on access to positions as army officers. An ordinance of 1579 attempted to place limitations on what the nobility considered to be an intrusion, by reserving positions as gendarmes of the guard for gentlemen who had served at least three years. Only "gentlemen-captains or outstanding soldiers" were admitted to the king's guard (the future bodyguard). This ordinance had little effect, and an edict issued in 1600 specified the admission into ordnance gendarme companies (heavy cavalry) of none but gentlemen or those who had served for ten years; the same rules applied to regimental officers. This edict attempted to put an end to the granting of noble status for military responsibilities carried out by one family for three generations.

The Michau Code of 1629 reveals that ideas changed little in the first part of the seventeenth century. On the one hand, the military profession still appeared to be linked with the nobility, since the hope was expressed that gentlemen should constitute at least a fourth of all military men (a condition that no longer held true even in the cavalry); and on the other hand, the code acknowledged the presence of soldiers of fortune who were officers without noble status. After 1635 the increase in the numbers of effectives destroyed all hope for the goal specified in the 1629 code.

In the period from 1661 to 1678, actual warfare together with the renown of the French armies drained the kingdom of all that the nobility could provide in the way of military men. It was difficult to proceed any further. Louis XIV had already called upon commoners for his guard, which had been reorganized in 1664 with the abolition of the sale of officers' posts within it. After 1684 the nobility could not furnish enough officers for the army, and it was necessary to attract men who lived like aristocrats and who could easily, because of their wealth, recruit and maintain companies. It was at this time that rivalry between aristrocrats and bourgeoisie arose in the army, in the competition for commissions. The old social framework did not change, for commoners who sought officer rank did so not as middle-class burghers but as aspiring noblemen. And the rivalry was still moderate under Louis XIV, as there were positions and promotions available for all gentlemen. The wars went on and on, and applicants for officers' posts grew scarce, for losses increased and money was lacking; it became an ever-greater burden to set up a son in the army. So the king had to order the provincial administrators (notably in 1704) to stimulate interest in military careers among those in their areas who lived like aristocrats. After 1692, it was necessary to give companies in newly formed regiments to commoners. When Louis XIV created the cadet companies in 1682, he expressed his desire to welcome young gentlemen into them, but he did not bar middle-class sons from entry if their families had the means to establish and keep them in service. Money played an ever-increasing part in the acquisition of commissions, and those nobles who were still wealthy profited by buying regiments, while the middle classes bought companies.

Many younger sons of nobles in legal or administrative positions, or young men from families who lived like nobles, were able to achieve honorable military careers under Louis XIV, although not necessarily rising to the highest levels (Saint-Simon's claims to the contrary notwithstanding). If Louis XIV allowed money to conflict with birth in the granting of officers' posts, he at least made an effort to maintain the element of merit in his decisions. The institution of a *cursus* for promotion based on the non-purchasable offices of lieutenant, re-formed captain, captain of grenadiers, major, lieutenant colonel, and brigadier, as well as the establishment of promotion schedules that took into account seniority and exceptional service, were intended primarily to keep open opportunities for noblemen who were not wealthy. The middle classes could benefit from these measures, but ennoblement for military service became rare at this time, and the creation of the Order of Saint Louis allowed for recompense without promotion or ennoblement.

Access to positions as general officers was possible for the lesser nobility, but advancement was fastest for those who could buy a company or a regiment. Thus under Louis XIV the proportion of field marshals who attained their positions by way of non-venal posts was one in three, and for lieutenant generals the proportion was only one in seven. The court nobility and the higher nobility had an advantage, then, particularly foreigners whom the king hoped to attract to his service. Titled nobility held 76 percent of the posts of lieutenant general, untitled nobility held only 16 percent, and men of doubtful noble status or commoners, only 8 percent. It is true that many of the titles had only recently been conferred on the title-holder. In fact, 4.8 percent of these positions were filled by the sons of bourgeois or professional families, 7.9 percent by men recently ennobled (a quarter of them by Colbert), 26.8 percent by men whose forebears had been granted titles in the sixteenth and seventeenth centuries, 25 percent by those whose noble status went back to the fourteenth and fifteenth centuries, and 43.6 percent by men whose ancestors had been noblemen before 1300. Court nobility and families with illustrious ancestors were favored, although half the generals had no active command and those who were really incapable were (apart from some regrettable exceptions) given no responsibilities at all. And families in which no one had actually achieved a general officer's position might rise to the social rank that accompanied such a position; this was true of about half the families in that rank. All these developments reflected the changing status of military families. Many foreigners were drawn to French service: about 15 percent of the lieutenant generals were from other countries, including eight Swiss, six Germans, three Italians, one Swede, and eight Englishmen, Scots, and Irishmen; most of them came to France in 1690.

It seems very likely that under Louis XIV, men who were déclassé—degraded from noble or bourgeois origins—associated with men of the popular elite without too much conflict, at subordinate-officer level; the hardships of a soldier's or a subordinate officer's life relegated social matters to second place. *Officiers de fortune* achieved a second-lieutenancy primarily through constant and dedicated service, and it is not certain whether gentlemen and middle-class sons were found more frequently than other classes among these *officiers de fortune*. Guards companies became steadily more open to the common people after 1664, when venality was abolished, and in 1690 the bodyguards were chosen from the best men in the cavalry regiments without regard to birth or wealth. In 1708 inquiry was limited to asking whether applicants had been servants. Thus even sons of laborers were admitted into the king's household troops.

The demobilization of Louis XIV's great army, which coincided with the reaction among the nobles during the Regency period, led to a reorganization among company officers and guards troops of non-noble origin. In 1718 certificates of nobility were required from all who applied for appointments as officers. This reaction did not last long, however. From 1726 on, commoners were admitted to newly organized cadet companies, and

in 1734, at the time of the War of the Polish Succession, intendants were again ordered to encourage enlistment by young gentlemen, noble or otherwise, who had at their disposal an income
of more than 400 livres. Motivation was no longer the same as it
had been under Louis XIV, however. The lesser nobility,
exhausted by the wars of the reign just past, found it more and
more difficult to maintain their positions; luxurious living became
important, and all advancement became blocked by men of the
highest birth, the sons of financiers, or nobles in legal or other
civilian professions, whose wealth allowed them to proceed
rapidly upward through the purchasable offices. There was no
lack of wealthy young burghers hoping to acquire brilliant repu-
tations so that their families could mingle with the nobility. At
mid-century, according to Tuetey, a third of the officers may
have had non-noble backgrounds. They were primarily in
subaltern-officer positions. *Officiers de fortune* represented a
minority among them, except in the cavalry, where officers from
the highest levels of the aristocracy preferred to have experienced
and dedicated lieutenants from the ranks, rather than young
bourgeois. Similarly, once the reaction of 1715 was over, the
guards companies, like all the troops of the king's household,
filled up with middle-class sons rather than provincial nobles or
men of the lowest classes, as life in these guards troops had become more costly than life as an infantry lieutenant.

There were still those who hoped to reconcile the old social
order with the new realities. The minister of war, Comte
d'Argenson, decided to renew the practice of granting noble
status in return for military service, a practice that had been
discouraged after 1600 and especially after 1680. The edict of 1750
concerning military nobility had only a slight effect: a few general
officers, some old officers who held the Cross of Saint Louis and
who belonged to families which included three generations of
captains, were ennobled. The *officiers de fortune* could seldom
meet all the necessary requirements. And it seemed hypocritical

in any case to continue to require certificates of nobility, verified by four gentlemen of one's province, from all officer-candidates. These certificates were often mere forms. Nevertheless, between 1752 and 1789, letters of approval were prepared for those who asked for them, testifying to thirty years of service, twenty at the level of captain; more favorable testimony was provided for those who had attained higher levels, whose fathers and grandfathers had been awarded the Cross, or whose careers had been interrupted by war injuries. Such letters meant lifelong status as a noble, and allowed the individual's grandson, with luck, to become one of the nobility as well, provided that all descendants achieved similar recognition.

The edict was received favorably on the whole, even by the nobility, whose interest in a military career was once more aroused, but in reality the lot of a non-noble officer grew worse toward the end of the reign of Louis XV. Aristocratic young officers more easily accepted an *officier de fortune* who was aware of his social inferiority than a young middle-class officer whose military experience was no greater than their own. Brutal attempts were made to force a young bourgeois to retire, and complaints were made about him to the colonels or even to the court. Officers of low social backgrounds served as scapegoats after the humiliation of Rossbach, as the Prussian victory was attributed not only to the genius of Frederick II and the organization of the Prussian army but also to the fact that nobles held nearly all the officers' positions in that army. After a decree of 1758, a reaction of nobles developed, based largely on the Prussian experience. Army inspectors were firmly reminded that they were supposed to refuse all officers' posts to anyone who could not provide a certificate of nobility. In the next year this requirement was extended to the militia, in an attempt to increase its prestige. Of all the suggestions made by the Chevalier d'Arc, the concept of an incompatibility between low birth and an officer's post was retained, while the idea of ennobling more low-born officers was rejected. The role of money was particularly affected, since the king reassumed control of his regiments and companies in 1762, and the purchase of positions was gradually abolished throughout the army after 1776. On the eve of the Revolution the king controlled half of the officer vacancies, and the other half were assigned according to seniority.

A reaction on the part of the nobility was also evident in the area of officer-training, which had become a major concern. Only young men who could produce the four patents of nobility were supposed to be admitted to the military school that was founded in 1751. In many cases, however, the authorities closed their eyes to violations. The militarization of the engineer and artillery branches, which had progressed steadily from 1693 to 1755, led to greater numbers of gentlemen in those branches; but the school at Mézières, founded for engineers in 1749, as well as artillery schools, admitted recently ennobled candidates and those with non-noble origins. This policy was discontinued at Mézières in 1772, and in 1767 and 1777 admission for these social groups at other engineer and artillery institutions became more difficult. The schools were now reserved for aristocrats and for the sons of superior officers or captains who held the Cross of Saint Louis. Finally, in 1781, the "Edict" of Ségur was issued in an attempt to do away with the purely formal (but not necessarily valid) certificates: it required that the original papers attesting to nobility be produced. This arrangement was soon standard in all arms of the service. In 1788 the requirements for the sons of holders of the Cross of Saint Louis were made still more strict. From 1777 on, to become a lieutenant in the guards it was necessary to prove three hundred years of noble ancestry. The creation of special insignia for gentlemen-cadets in 1776, and then of a training unit for them in 1788, contributed to the trend. Young aristocrats were unquestionably subjected to more arduous studies and duties, but this did not appease the bitterness occasioned by these unwise policies.

Resentment was manifested at all levels. It was expressed when the estates-general were convened, in records of complaints by the nobility and by representatives of the third estate as well, revealing that the latter group no longer considered armed service to be an aristocratic monopoly. The gap was widened between the court nobility and other nobles after the standardization of presentation at court in 1760. The practice of granting colonels' positions at a very young age ("colonels in bibs") to members of families that had been received at court went back many years, although the most scandalous instances were eliminated by the end of the eighteenth century. It nevertheless became more and more difficult for the lesser nobility to exceed the level of lieutenant colonel. Indeed an ordinance passed in 1781 required most applicants to have spent twenty-five years in service as captain and carried out the functions of major, while a high-born young aristocrat could become a second-level colonel and six years later a commanding colonel simply by being twenty-three years old and having spent eight years in service as second lieutenant and lieutenant. In 1788 the level of brigadier, through which many of the lesser nobility rose to higher ranks, was abolished. There were still, however, some men of middle-class origins among the general officers, men who had begun their careers early in the reign of Louis XV. They were called "general officers of fortune."

Banned from the highest ranks, the lesser nobility opposed—with a bitterness all the greater—all access by wealthy commoners to company-officer (or higher) rank. Nevertheless, in 1789 about 10 percent of the some 10,000 army officers were still men of common birth, both bourgeois sons and soldiers of fortune. Their only hope of distinction lay in obtaining the Cross of Saint Louis at the age of sixty or so. The situation was only a little better in the technical branches, where non-noble officers were wealthy and educated bourgeois. Although they constituted as many as 25 percent of the active officers, their further promotion was made impossible, as young aristocrats, often poor, worked very hard at their studies and counted on being rewarded for their efforts. A study of the aristocrats in the army must take into account those who enlisted among the troops without indicating their status, only revealing it when asking for leave—which they then obtained easily—as their presence was regarded as strange, even suspicious. These slightly disgraceful gentlemen, who are not mentioned by social theorists studying the aristocracy, numbered some 3,000 in the French army on the eve of the Revolution.

Young middle-class men who were interested in pursuing a military career had to be satisfied with subordinate-officer positions. This situation explains the large number of subordinate officers who became excellent generals in the Revolution and under the Empire. It is interesting to observe that the recruitment chart for these men is closer to that for noncommissioned officers than to that for second lieutenants or lieutenants in the ancien regime. The explanation is that, after Choiseul, sergeants had to know how to read and write—a requirement that seemed less justified then than now. The men of the popular elite who until that time could rise to the ranks of the lower officers now found themselves barred from anything higher than corporal. At this level, a great social distance separated sergeants like Hoche, who was the son of a guard of the royal kennels, or Marceau, the son of a district prosecutor, from the son of a miller, like Stofflet, who never exceeded the level of corporal. Just as birth barred the way for skills without birth, so skills barred the way for merit without skills. Each level became isolated, then, shut in by envy for superiors and scorn for inferiors. The sum of all these antagonisms formed the basis for the social crisis in the French army just before the Revolution.

9

Special Characteristics of Military Societies

IN THE PRECEDING chapters we have seen that the groups of men constituting European armies possessed qualities, attitudes, and concerns that varied from one state to another. Their characters were affected both by the positions within the governments that were assigned to them by the sovereigns, and—even more often—by changes taking place within whole societies. And, when we consider the wide gap that separated officers from soldiers in the permanent armies, it is difficult to use an expression like "military society."

Nevertheless, civilians and military men became increasingly distinct, one from the other, during the eighteenth century. Military personnel were set apart from civilian society by their dwelling places, their clothes, their style of life, traditions, and codes of behavior. A clearly military identity marked a man for life, and sometimes his descendants as well. As officers became professionals, they became still more immersed in a military society, and the uniform—common to both officers and men—became a symbol of this social unit. The increasing importance of the technical aspects of military arts, together with the frequent conflicts, led to a constant exchange of innovation in strategic and tactical armament and instruction. In turn, military methods and ideas conditioned men. One could say that Gonzalo de Cór-

171

doba or Louvois, just as much as Frederick II, belong to the military history of all the European States. The armies became more and more alike. And so we can, after all, speak of a European military society.

These diverging tendencies, toward uniformity and toward distinguishable national traits, eventually came into conflict at a moral or psychological level, and it was this conflict that created favorable ground for the military insurrections in France in 1790 and the military collapse in Prussia in 1806. It is important, then, to identify the factors that led to cohesion within military societies, the behavior and codes of such societies, and the attitudes of their members toward civilians.

THE GROWING COHESION WITHIN MILITARY SOCIETIES

The term "cohesion" may be a little startling, when applied to armies with high rates of desertion, but we should note that desertions took place primarily among those who had been forcibly recruited and who had no military vocation, among them petty thieves and vagrants (who incidentally were good fighters). Even good soldiers were not above the temptation to quit after ill treatment, a quarrel, some humiliation, or in a fit of anger. Desertion sometimes acted like a contagious disease among compatriots or comrades; it particularly affected men in good health; 40 percent of the deserters were from twenty-one to twenty-five, often from frontier provinces; and it was at its highest rate in summer. In spite of the trouble it caused, desertion had the effect of selection, and we can perceive that within each company there existed a core of loyal men, with a fluctuating fringe of others. Cohesion can be seen as the result of control within these loyal cores. The conditioning brought about by such control was often powerful enough to create solid ties between men of diverse origins, including those who had been conscripted as well as those who had voluntarily enlisted.

Let us look at some characteristics of these social groups. In the Prussian and Russian armies military service lasted, theoretically, until death (or desertion). In Russia illness did not return a soldier to civilian status. In all countries some old soldiers were kept on, but in the western armies soldiers who had been wounded or who became ill were sent home. In the seventeenth century the re-forming of a regiment or a company resulted in the dismissal of men, and a soldier could negotiate with his captain for leave or dismissal. In France these arrangements were changed by Louvois. A citizen now enlisted to serve the king rather than a captain, and he could be transferred from a dispersed company to one that had been retained. Enlistment terms were set in 1682 at a minimum of six years and changed in 1762 to eight years. Dismissal was allowed only in peacetime, in the winter months, and at a rate of three from a company at one time. On the other hand, some secured an early dismissal by "buying" themselves out or by providing two replacements, and in fact service could actually last anywhere from a few weeks to several decades. The average term settled down to around six years, although for those who made up the central cores of the companies it was naturally considerably longer. It is interesting to note that men from rural backgrounds generally served longer than city men; although it was more difficult to attract them to the army, they stayed in more willingly. It is likely that these observations, made on the basis of a study of the French army, are to some extent valid for most of the western armies.

The demographic details of the military society are of course very diffierent from those for other groups. Even in peacetime, mortality was high when we remember that we are considering young men: 34 percent in the Vivarais infantry regiment between 1716 and 1749, for example. Not surprisingly, it was higher in wartime but, contrary to expectations, battle was not the principal cause. We will set aside for the moment the fictitious deaths of deserters, whom the captains listed as killed in order to be able to find replacements at the king's expense, and whose disappearance made losses seem to be much greater than they actually were. The real killer was the winter quarters. Armies carried epidemics about, fevers called "military fevers" in a corruption of the term "miliary fever" (an epidemic disease characterized by fever and skin lesions). The youngest soldiers were the most susceptible, and a quarter of the deaths caused by disease took place during the first year of service—one more factor that helped to strengthen the unity of the central core in each company.

The military society was by nature one of soldiers—adult single males. It included civilians as well, however: provisioners, carters, servants, some women (often wives of subordinate officers or of older soldiers), and children. Servants were found especially in the cavalry, where they were sometimes more numerous than military men early in the seventeenth century. They became fewer after that, although some superior officers maintained a large household, particularly in the French army.

The armies of the Latin countries had the fewest married men, under 10 percent in the Castilian *tercios* but 15 to 30 percent in the low-German or Walloon *tercios*, in the early 1600s. Women and children were by far the most numerous in the armies with the longest terms of service. During the Thirty Years War a soldier was free to marry in Germany, and in 1660 bachelors in the Spandau garrison were only 30 percent. Military authorities recognized that some women were required in each company to wash and mend clothes, but they took measures to avoid having too many married men in order that the armies might not be burdened with responsibility for a great number of non-combatants, and so that discipline might be maintained. Marriage for the soldiers, however, was felt to be the best means to limit prostitution in the camps.

The Great Elector hoped to limit the proportion of married men in each corps to 30 or 40 percent. Frederick William I allowed only three married men per company, unless the prospective wife could furnish 300 florins. But it was difficult to maintain such restrictions among the Kantonists. The Berlin garrison in 1777 included 30 percent married men; 40 percent of those on leave were married. By 1802 there were in the Prussian army approximately 59,000 wives and 78,000 children for every 100,000 men who were the king's subjects; for foreigners the figure was 36,000 wives and 49,000 children for 100,000 soldiers. At the end of the eighteenth century the English army also appears to have included many married men. The situation was very different in France, where scarcely more than 15 percent of the soldiers admitted to the Invalides hospital were married. Of course all wives did not follow along with their husbands in the regiments.

The number of children was relatively low, not surprisingly if we consider the hardships and epidemics of camp life. Moreover, many children were turned over to families at home or abandoned. Indeed, it required a certain patience, on the part of the authorities and the soldiers both, to keep the children in the units. It became possible to inscribe on the company registers so-called "children of the corps," or "hopeful children," that is, those for whom rapid growth to maturity was expected. There is an implication that comrades shared responsibility for these children as long as they were dependent, probably in exchange for small services and a percentage of any wages earned.

A recognizable social policy developed in the eighteenth century, first in the German armies. In Prussia women living with the troops were divided into three groups according to their needs: each month they were granted twelve or six groschen, or none, plus four groschen per child. Widows often married another soldier of the same company, and in 1747 a widow's pension was instituted in Bavaria. For a long time only the foreign regiments in France granted funds to soldiers' wives, and even then only a few were assisted. The practice was extended to other corps in the late eighteenth century. Some care was provided for male orphans, in the hope of raising them to be soldiers. Orphanages were founded in Bavaria in 1683, in Potsdam in 1722, in Saxony in 1738, and in Austria. The emperor Joseph II established for each regiment a house in which forty-eight soldiers' children were raised and educated. Steps were taken in France toward entering on the payroll at half-pay two children per company. And schools for army children were established by the Chevalier Paulet and the Duc de Liancourt, with the approval of the government.

The presence of women and children turned some armies into true societies. This was of course the case in military posts in the frontier territories of the Hapsburg monarchy, and even more so for Cossack units. In Prussian garrisons the regiment formed in effect a parish, in which the chaplain performed funeral services, weddings, and baptisms, and kept a "parish" register.

Even where married soldiers were less common, the army formed a kind of social unit in which regiments and companies corresponded to provinces and villages, with some fixed members and a certain number of temporary ones. The solidarity of these units stemmed not only from discipline; it was the result, too, of personal relationships between soldiers, or between a captain and his men, and it was based on loyalty and comradeship. Cohesion was especially strong wherever recruiting had retained a seigniorial flavor. At a higher level, despite a fairly localized recruitment base for some corps (particularly in the Austrian army), armies brought about a certain fusion between men of diverse provincial and social backgrounds, a unity that gave them a truly national character. The kingdom of Prussia, and later the Austrian empire, owed a great deal to their armies in this respect.

COLLECTIVE BEHAVIOR

The armies of the sixteenth century, with their very low proportions of permanent soldiers, were very different from the armies of the late eighteenth century, in which the number of men serving on a permanent basis was high. It is possible to envision a contrast between "soldier armies" on the one hand and "automaton armies" on the other. But such an opposition is too simple, and in any case the evolution from one to the other was long as well as complex.

Collective responses on the part of soldiers were often evoked by decisions concerning discipline or wages, and thus by matters of governmental power: authority and finance. The *tercio* provides an illustration of the willingness in the sixteenth century to accept discipline and individual sacrifices for the sake of a collective glory and the national cause. We have already seen that in the second half of the seventeenth century discipline became generally more strict in the West and wages were paid more regularly, at least in peacetime. Bad conditions at the end of the seventeenth century, however, led to mutinies; during the 1600s and early 1700s there were many desertions; after the middle of the eighteenth century there were serious "epidemics" of *nostalgie*, or homesickness.

Mutinies were more often set off by delays in pay, lack of food, or some act on the part of an unpopular leader that led to resentment, than by exhausting fighting. They took the form of uprisings and strikes. Parker records forty-five mutinies in the Spanish army in Flanders alone between 1572 and 1607; twenty-one of these took place between 1596 and 1607. Some lasted a year or longer. Mutineers had specific goals, and they elected leaders (*Ambosat* for the Germans, *electo* for the Spanish) to negotiate with commanding officers. Mutiny broke out most often among the lowest-paid men, pikemen or harquebusiers, but if the colonel was not able to isolate the leaders the mutiny could spread throughout the entire regiment. Officers and soldiers who did not join would be expelled. Lieutenants participated on an equal footing with the men. Mutineers would secure a stronghold and then organize themselves into a unit. The "Republic of Hoogstraten" lasted from 1602 to 1605. Such groups levied "taxes" on the local inhabitants. Return to order might be achieved after meetings at which the mutineers would demand pardon, payment of back wages, and sometimes a general muster during which each soldier could choose the unit he wanted to join. It is interesting to observe that the mutineers never had a revolutionary or social program, and that there were no general mutinies. The mutineer continued to be regarded as a soldier, and those who remained loyal usually refused to oppose him. In the Spanish army in Flanders mutinies ceased after 1607 because of better management of the distribution of food, wages, and marching schedules; in the seventeenth and eighteenth centuries mutinies became unusual. They might have political motives (for example, the revolt of the parliamentary forces in England in 1647), or stem from protest against being sent overseas (as in the insurrection of the Royal-Comtois regiment in 1772).

Desertion, rife in the sixteenth century, became more disruptive than mutiny at the time of the Thirty Years War. Setting aside multiple-enlistment "desertions," let us examine the ways in which men reacted to temptations to desert. Like mutiny, desertion was a "collective" evil that most strongly affected the lowest-paid groups. It was caused more often by discontentment than by fear, and in the early seventeenth century, groups of thirty to a hundred men, following elected leaders, sometimes deserted. Men frequently deserted after a highly productive raid that allowed them to return as rich men to civilian life, though few were clever enough to maintain their status there and many re-enlisted under another ruler. And desertion was often the result of deliberate seduction. In the eighteenth century, examples of collective desertion were still to be found, often among soldiers who were serving unwillingly, for example, those French prisoners conscripted by Frederick II who deserted en masse. To avoid this the Austrian army created garrison battalions of foreigners or deserters, units that were easy to keep under surveillance. Militiamen seldom deserted in groups except during the

War of the Spanish Succession; usually they disappeared before reaching their units. After 1650 desertion became largely an individual act, rarely involving more than two or three men; usually fellow-soldiers kept quiet and captains did little about it.

The success of the campaign against desertion led to the appearance of another problem, that of homesickness, which was much in evidence in the second half of the eighteenth century. Doctors viewed it as an illness, whose victim lost appetite and had no energy or will. This *mal du pays* particularly attacked mountain men or any who were isolated by extreme dialects; it was less common in reserve units, but when it did appear in such units it was likely to be more contagious.

The changing forms of resistance to discipline, from mutiny to desertion to homesickness, reveal the growing power of such discipline over the individual.

Commentaries on the moral behavior of the troops are on the whole very critical. Provincial administrators were almost wholly occupied with the difficulties caused by the presence of troops in their districts, and as administrative activity grew, authorities tightened requirements concerning the conduct of the soldiers. Officers often added their complaints to those of civil authorities, but they tended to report only those offenses that might threaten military discipline. An esprit de corps often inclined them to qualify as "harmless errors" certain offenses that caused suffering for civilians, while the same acts would be judged more severely when their victim was a military person. In matters of custom or manners, the dividing lines were even less clear, and officers attempted to shield their men from prosecution by civilian courts.

Violence, licentious behavior, and looting were the factors most often mentioned. Duels between officers—or between soldiers—became rare in the eighteenth century, but they did not completely disappear. Riots among the men were frequent, and group loyalties sometimes turned them into large-scale battles. Rowdy behavior was looked on with some tolerance, and drunkenness was rife in all armies (although it was reduced in the French army in the late 1700s). Wild sprees were frequent, and despite rigorous measures prostitution continued to thrive near the camps, especially in the armies in which few men were married. In France Louvois, the War Council during the Regency, and the ministers of the second half of the eighteenth century took strong measures to make the problem at least less obvious, and similar action was taken in Prussia by Frederick William I and in Austria under Maria Theresa. Gambling was universal among officers and men and frequently caused poverty and disgrace. Finally, stealing was prevalent in all armies. At best, energetic officers could keep it within certain limits. But it adversely affected troop loyalty and cohesion, driving men apart, as was the case in the Austrian army during the War of the Austrian Succession. Frenchmen in particular had a reputation among the western armies of being pilferers.

The cultural level of the troops was generally low. At all times men of wealthy and respected backgrounds were to be found among the troops, but of course education was not always an accurate indication of military worthiness. Cultural levels appear to have risen in the West by the late eighteenth century, particularly in the French army, where the social crisis pushed gentlemen back to subordinate-officer levels, and middle-class men—sometimes college-educated—to noncommissioned-officer positions. We lack statistical measures for the levels of education among the troops, except for the corps in which men had to sign the register on enlisting (as was true for the troops of the *Compagnie des Indes* in France) or for the Swiss troops, who had to sign on a special register for all sums received. It appears from parish records, however, that the percentage of soldiers who could sign their names was lower than the percentage for the civilian population. This impression may be inaccurate. Indeed, if men did not exactly learn to write in the regiments, at least they often learned to sign their names. Moreover, there is no doubt that a tour of duty in the army, in the second half of the eighteenth century, helped to refine the manners of many recruits.

For a long time the leisure activities of the soldiers revealed a general intellectual poverty, but by the eighteenth century the troops spent their evenings much as did the peaceful country people. The tavern nevertheless remained the most important diversion, but it became increasingly a place for men of equal rank to meet. Officers, noncommissioned officers, and men each had their own taverns. In some Prussian towns soldiers could only use certain mugs, which were hung up at the doors of the inns. Public places were often closed to soldiers, but in garrison towns the men could work for townsmen and make "contacts" in that way. Although garrison life was hardly conducive to it, some officers and even noncommissioned officers could read. Some were Freemasons or formed military lodges. Noncommissioned officers could only belong as servant-brothers.

Although military authorities felt that religion was one element of discipline, the troops formed a nucleus of irreligion in many countries. Often cited as exemplary, undoubtedly because they were exceptional, were the crusading faith of the first army of Gustavus Adolphus and the religious fervor of the victors at White Mountain. Even during the religious wars, tolerance increased within the troops after a few campaigns. It was essential in some of the German armies. Usually it was part of a general absence of rigidity. Even the clergy, in the Latin countries at least, scarcely attempted to guide the spiritual lives of the soldiers. Military chaplains were sometimes the very worst members of the secular clergy. Some monastic orders devoted themselves to the task, however, as friars, in the north of France and the Netherlands. The Prussian kings gave more attention to the problem. Superstition, which had prevailed to a serious extent in the armies of the Thirty Years War, ceased at least to be a paralyzing force in the western armies during the eighteenth century. Church service was often the only religious practice. At Chambord Maurice de Saxe, a Lutheran, marched his men (among whom were some Moslems) summarily to Mass.

The French army was probably the one in which religious laxity was the most widespread. With its foreign regiments it included a greater proportion of Protestants than did the nation as a whole. The number of Huguenots in French units was temporarily reduced by the revocation of the Edict of Nantes; later, the army served as a means of escape for those who were trying to get to another country, and eventually as a refuge from prosecution. For many reasons, then, the observation of religious practices other than Mass became difficult in the eighteenth century, and irreligion was widespread.

In considering collective behavior we must not forget those factors that contributed to a sense of honor, loyalty to comrades, and an esprit de corps. For example, soldiers often forced their officers to expel a man for "low" behavior, perhaps for having mistreated a comrade or for having given a bad impression of the military valor of the corps.

In assessing behavior in combat we find that bravery was possessed equally by officers and men, even among the militiamen. We can discern, however, both enthusiasm and panic, the latter usually limited. A stirring appeal to patriotic sentiments that emphasized the "gaming" aspects of war, scorn for the enemy, the arrival or prospect of provisions, the impatience of units waiting for their chance to attack—all these could inspire zeal. On the other hand, inadequate supplies, rumors of negotiations, a lack of confidence in leaders, fatigue, a feeling of insecurity within a unit driven from a stronghold, or a surprise attack might cause panic. Even elite troops were susceptible to this, perhaps because so much was expected from them or because their numbers included young men looking for social glory rather than for opportunities to fight. Enthusiasm and panic were of course contagious, but loyalty to the unit tended to reinforce discipline and inspire emulation. If much foolish behavior stemmed from the esprit de corps, it was the source of often unrecognized loyalty and sacrifice as well.

A MILITARY ETHIC

From 1500 to 1800 an evolution from a "warrior" mentality to an "army" mentality took place. We see evidence of this in the conception of honor and the idea of the hero, and in changing manifestations of hero-worship. Two questions we will attempt to answer are: How did the new attitude differ among officers and men? Did it assume different aspects in the various armies of western Europe?

The modern era retained some of the morality of chivalry, keeping alive the medieval romances that were still fashionable everywhere in the sixteenth century; although anachronistic, they continued to be widely read. The warrior mentality was largely an aristocratic one that presented the foot soldier, if at all, as crude and violent more often than courageous.

But in the sixteenth century, changes were taking place in representations of military types. The example of the Spanish generals—among others Gonzalo de Córdoba, the "Great Captain"—contributed to this; and in France, Montluc and Brantôme were writing of virtues that were not precisely those of a knight: sturdiness, endurance, experience, sangfroid now opposed the generous but impulsive actions of the knight. We can identify several reasons for this transformation of the warrior ideal: among them are the greater number of fighting men, who no longer acknowledged the profession of arms to be a monopoly of an elite, and the increasing role of infantry in battle. The use of firearms naturally gave rise to new, less individual, forms of combat. And with the Renaissance, the ideas of ancient Rome dominated military literature for three centuries. Until the nineteenth century the model for the fighting man was to be the Roman legionnaire. This conception, along with the growth of an esprit de corps, led to the uniting of soldier and officer under a single ethical code.

The Wars of Religion and the Thirty Years War, meanwhile, did not always produce the model fighting man. The Baroque age was one of duels, wild and ruffianly conduct, and a resurgence of violent impulsiveness, and there was less of the trust that Montluc hoped to see prevail between soldiers and their leaders: it became difficult to maintain a single moral code for the two groups. Honor took on a social meaning, and a distinction was made between a gentleman's honor and a soldier's honor. The nobleman was seeking personal glory, but when it came to goals both officer and soldier were after profit.

But the idea of the soldier gained favor in the next century. The terms *soudoyer, soudard, soldato,* soldier, all originally referred simply to fighting men who received a *solde,* or wage. In French the term *soldat* acquired a more honorable sense in the middle of the sixteenth century, and other European languages followed suit in the seventeenth century. The technical term, mercenary, took on some of the scorn attached to the *solde,* and the term *soudard* continued in use, now associated with the fear and hatred inspired by the behavior of hardened, violent men of war. Brantôme could write, around 1600, of the "fine title of soldier." In military language the word "soldier" no doubt retained the narrow sense of foot soldier or the somewhat broader one of man of the troops. In the early seventeenth century it still held a social connotation: ordinances used the expression "gentlemen and soldiers" to designate all men of war, a usage that denied any possibility of association of soldiers with the ranks of the aristocracy. Under Louis XIV the expression "officers and soldiers" was used—a term referring now only to rank. Meanwhile, the word "soldier" had taken the place of "man of war" used in a favorable sense. Any man of war who was brave and who knew his trade well was called a soldier, and after 1700 a gentleman or an outstanding officer would be called "a good soldier." This new usage blurred the idea of a particular status to the extent that in France during the eighteenth century the term "*militaire*" was used as a noun to designate all men serving under the French flag, in peacetime even more often than in times of war.

This semantic evolution reveals the stages in the change from the warrior mentality to the military mentality that was tending to become common to officers and soldiers alike. Such a tendency was far from universal, however. In Prussia a soldier was taught to fear his officer more than the enemy, and in England the division persisted as well. The barrier between officers and soldiers, in terms of a military ethic, was probably less substantial in the Austrian and French armies, except for those cases where the Prussian model was deliberately imitated.

Among military virtues emphasis was particularly placed on discipline for all—officers and soldiers—and on the spirit of sacrifice. In the 1600s whenever a soldier's life was exalted great emphasis was given to the weariness and bloodshed endured, and a soldier's death was a glorious heroic event. In the 1700s, such a death was a sacrifice. Heroism had changed its meaning as well, taking on a new role in military training. The death of the Chevalier Bayard [one of the knights of Charlemagne], which was often held up as an example in the sixteenth and early seventeenth centuries, was the culmination of a long series of individual heroic exploits. In the eighteenth century, the death of the Chevalier d'Assas [who died a hero's death in 1760, while alerting his troops to danger] was the type for death-as-sacrifice. D'Assas and Sergeant Dubois gave their lives in obscure circumstances, without using their weapons. They were otherwise unknown, and their humble heroism seemed to be within the reach of men of all ranks, in contrast to Bayard's death, which was of a kind reserved for the elite. This idea of sacrifice under discipline, now called for in the military profession, is expressed, too, in the moving song by Uhland, "Der gute Kamerad." The soldier, who sees his best friend fall at his feet, can only spare him a glance, as he must quickly reload his gun. After the last third of the eighteenth century, the germ of the mentality of Vigny's *Servitude et grandeur militaires* (see p. 103) can be discerned.

This submission to discipline, which was required by military techniques that were becoming increasingly complex and which controlled the men's very reflexes, tended to differentiate military men from civilians at a moment when armies were more and more often made up of militiamen or conscripts.

The western armies retained some elements of the discipline that had been imposed by the chivalric code on officers and men. Among these were the rules of war that forbade victors to kill wounded or unarmed men and required them to treat prisoners well, to respect the terms of surrender, and to leave the civilian population out of the war. But these rules were difficult to impose. Some leaders felt that they should not be applied at the cost of their own men's safety. As late as the seventeenth century many were reluctant to keep prisoners if they threatened to become a burden or even a danger to the rearguard troops, above all when supplies were low. By the eighteenth century, however, prisoners were only rarely killed. The conventional rules of war did not obtain for those who broke them, and the fear of reprisals helped limit savagery on the part of the soldiers. Progress was made toward "humanizing" war during the conflicts of the eighteenth century, at least in the West.

Such benefits did not apply to civilians who engaged in acts of war. Up to the War of the Spanish Succession and later still, in the wars of the Revolution, governments called upon native populations to resist invaders. Military leaders considered it their duty to protect their men from surprise attacks by civilian snipers, who were not soldiers in the eyes of such leaders. When such attacks were made, reprisals were often carried out. Here again the military morality was distinct from the general morality.

A distinction was evident, too, in matters of religion, particularly in attitudes toward death. The Church conceded that killing was part of the soldier's duties and could not by itself mean perdition for him. Yet it was necessary to die in a state of grace, and the chevalier was supposed to make confession and take communion before combat. The increase in numbers of fighting men made individual absolution impossible for most, and chaplains granted collective absolutions in the form of blessings after Mass. Protestant armies also held benediction services for the troops, often with hymns. As death could come unexpectedly, however, it was agreed that these various collective absolutions remained valid for a certain length of time. It can be seen that such laxity was hardly conducive to the inclusion of rigorous religious practices in the military ethic, but religious ceremonies with a military character evolved for the troops: the presentation of arms at the consecration of the bread and wine, a bugle fanfare for the elevation of the host, and so forth.

Funeral services for soldiers also illustrate the evolution of the military ethic. In the Middle Ages they were universally Christian; truces were negotiated after battles so that the dead could be buried. The Renaissance reintroduced rituals from Roman antiquity, like marching past with reversed arms, and the practice of firing a salute spread from Italy. In the Baroque era, funeral services for leaders became very complicated, but while rites became more dramatic all over Europe, the burying of soldiers in the midst of wars was often carried out with no individual blessing at all. It was not until the reign of Louis XIV that a single fairly simple ritual was established for both officers and men. The degree of importance of the unit determined the proper honors, and the number of volleys fired varied according to the rank of the deceased. The ceremony was always conducted by a military man of the same rank, or by a corporal for enlisted men. But these customs were followed only in the eighteenth century, and only when circumstances permitted.

Although the services for officers and soldiers became more alike in detail, this was not true for tombs and funerary monuments, which continued to be reserved for noble families and

officers who were to be especially honored by the ruler. Gentlemen were provided with tombs that reflected their military calling
even if their actual careers had been undistinguished. Martial
symbols and representations of combats multiplied during the
Renaissance. Turenne's tomb, first constructed at Saint-Denis,
set a sober, grandiose style that was to be imitated for a century.
There was, however, nothing to distinguish a soldier's tomb,
when he received one, from graves of the very poorest folk. In
memorial chapels built at the sites of victories, the officers were
listed by name, but only a general allusion was made to the men.
The French Revolution sought to merge all forms of homage into
a single form for all ranks, singling out only those men who had
been especially heroic. At the end of the eighteenth century that
goal had not yet been reached, as the wars of the Empire revealed.

MILITARY MEN AND CIVILIANS

Earlier in this study we dealt with the attitudes of civilians
toward military men. To be considered here are the reactions of
soldiers toward civilians. First the behavior of officers and men in
individual dealings with civilians will be examined; then we will
look for evidence of a communal attitude within the army as a
whole, as it undertook the tasks assigned to it in the various
countries. It will be useful, too, to inquire into the status of the
former soldier in society and the role that he might find for himself. It is in France, where the Revolution and the military coup
d'état of Brumaire [elevating Napoleon to power in 1799] took
place, that these questions have received the most attention.

For a long time there was no indication that a military gentleman (authentic or self-styled), living part of the year at home with
his family, looked with disfavor on members of the military aristocracy who were not actually in service. If there was any disdain
it was felt by hereditary aristocrats toward other nobles. Gentlemen who left the army did not feel that they had put aside their

arms or that they had sunk to a lower social level. But the professionalization of the officers' corps brought about a change in this view in Prussia—and, by the end of the eighteenth century, elsewhere as well, wherever the Prussian model was imitated. The Chevalier d'Arc [writing in the 1750s] would have liked to see officer-nobles who abandoned the army deprived of their noble status.

The adoption of uniforms and the housing of troops in barracks in garrison towns strongly influenced officers' attitudes, except for those who were members of the court nobility. In the late 1700s a French officer in winter quarters was no longer so eager to put off his uniform as he had been in the reign of Louis XIV. Similarly, we observe that more officers' wives lived at least part of the year in the towns where their husbands were stationed. Coffee houses, clubs, and Masonic lodges in such towns allowed some contacts with local bourgeois society. An officer was possibly less shut out from civilian society than he was to be in France during most of the nineteenth century. But in all these contacts his identity as a military man was being more clearly defined.

It was the same for the men. Under Louis XV civilians became used to having the troops among them, but the increase in the policy of housing soldiers in barracks, together with strong control, isolated the soldier to a greater extent and also made him less interested in inspiring fear and more conscious that he was a being different from a civilian, one who was contributing to public order and the authority of the State.

From the earliest times the army had been used by rulers to put down political revolts, but it was seldom the first resort. Under traditional arrangements a ruler was protected by a bodyguard; in France a royal household force was created from a sizable number of elite troops, and this was imitated in other countries. The king's household troops were responsible for the "security" surrounding the king, his palace, and his capital city. In the rest of the kingdom, maintaining order (an anachronistic term, incidentally) fell to governors and their guard troops, and above all to the town militias. The king would send a few units from his household troops if it appeared necessary. In cases of widespread revolt, however, the king reacted as he would for a foreign war: he announced a general emergency and levied troops. If he had permanent troops on hand, he assigned some units to the area concerned. As it happened, civil wars often arose at a time when a foreign war had taken troops elsewhere (for example, the French Wars of Religion, the Fronde, the revolt of the Camisards, and uprisings in Hungary); or in the late eighteenth century a civil war was likely to set off a larger crisis (the American Revolution, the revolt in the Austrian Netherlands). Popular uprisings were approached in the same manner, but as a rule order had already been re-established by the time the royal troops arrived. The suppression of the *Papier timbré* revolt in 1675 revealed the degree of effectiveness that could be expected from the army. There were no more uprisings of this magnitude in France until 1789.

Meanwhile, the large numbers of men in service, their distribution throughout all areas until the middle of the eighteenth century, and their mobility turned the troops into an instrument for maintaining order at a time when the town militias were becoming more and more reluctant to assume their police role. Soldiers in garrison towns were found guarding public buildings or keeping order at public ceremonies, or even making rounds as nightwatchmen. They were called on to put down urban riots as well, but it should be said that, although officers and men carried out such duties regularly, they did so with growing reluctance, at least in France. The regiment of French guards complained of being constantly kept on the alert for police duties.

The French king withdrew his troops from this role to an increasing extent. By 1720 the mounted constabulary forces had been "militarized," and after the Seven Years War the town police forces were in turn put on a military footing: the Paris guard was reorganized in 1764, and royal watch companies were established in principal cities. Toward the end of the century these police forces and the household force were apparently strong enough for the king to be able to send his army away from Paris, except for a few garrison battalions. In 1785, 103 infantry regiments out of 106 were at the frontier, and the three others were stationed more than fifty leagues from the capital. A single cavalry regiment was stationed nearby, at Melun. When some regiments were recalled too late to Paris in 1789, they were unfamiliar with the city and were no longer accustomed to suppressing riots. The French guards became a kind of security force, remaining loyal up to the moment when they went over as a bloc to the Revolution. Only the king's household troops remained faithful to Louis XVI until the end.

At the time when society was basically military in nature, and when the distinction between civilians and military men was less pronounced, troops of hired soldiers did not hesitate to fight anyone who was pointed out as the enemy, whoever it might be. But the evolution of the idea of the "nation," together with the professionalization of the army, produced officers and soldiers who were willing to defend the country against foreign attack but more and more reluctant to enforce order among civilians. It was admittedly difficult to distinguish between "preventive" and "repressive" operations. There was probably more hesitation on the part of the professional officer to fight against Frenchmen in the Vendée in 1793 than there had been to contend with the Camisards in the first decade of the century.

On the eve of the Revolution, French soldiers were not eager to act as praetorian guards, and in 1789 they frequently considered themselves fairly close to the civilians in sympathy, despite their physical separation from them. Officers willing to play the role of political instruments were lacking, above all. But it should be remembered that isolation and strict discipline had raised the possibility that military men might become tools of government, if a common motive had been present.

Did the army play a political role? We see many instances of rulers using their own armed forces to suppress opposition. One case was Charles I's forceful action against five members of the English Parliament in 1642; another was Pierre Broussel's arrest, ordered by Anne of Austria in 1648. Sometimes there was a broader purpose: in 1650 William II of Orange used military force in an attempt to strengthen the powers of the stadholder in Holland. In 1772 Gustavus III of Sweden, with the help of his troops, succeeded in limiting the powers of the *Riksdag*. And, finally, in July 1789 Louis XVI brought troops to Paris for a military stand, confused and badly prepared though it was. It is interesting to observe that in the West these *coups de force* usually failed. In contrast, the Russian army was called in on many occasions by one or another candidate for the throne who hoped to hasten the process of succession by deposing the sovereign (in 1741, 1762, and 1801). In all these cases the army's role was simply that of an instrument for a coup d'état.

Did military leaders take on political roles? To answer this question we must look at the men who held high places in government. In the sixteenth and early seventeenth century military men played political roles or led uprisings. There were great men, like Francis de Guise or Gaspard de Coligny, who profited from their military successes and took over the leadership of a political or religious party; or princes like William of Orange who were called upon to direct a popular revolt; or political leaders who became soldiers, like Cromwell; or ambitious men pursuing personal goals: princes like Henri de Guise or Condé, generals like Wallenstein, military leaders thoroughly experienced in handling public disorders, like Turenne, Lambert, Monck. Such men used their own troops or raised others.

We see in the English Revolution the outstanding example of an army that was not content to be an instrument and so took over a political role for itself, adopting a political program and organization that it imposed on the country. This case was perhaps unique in the ancien regime. After the flare-up of military ambitions in the middle 1600s, the army did not have a political role of its own in France until the time of the Directory. Was the situation under the Directory brought about by the changes that took place in the army during the last years of the ancien regime?

It is a difficult question to answer. The military rebellions of 1790 must of course be seen in connection with the general unrest, but they were stimulated also by the professional claims of the soldiers; when the soldiers lifted themselves above the level of their specific demands it was to express ideas that were not their own. There was no precedent in the French ancien regime for the political role played by the army under the Directory. But we should not overlook the conviction held by the officers that they formed a special force within the nation; they were reluctant to engage in police tasks; and they were confident that they were serving the best interests of the nation as well as defending it from foreign attack. Under a king who was not interested in military matters, the Council of War formed in 1788 played a decidedly political part; it did not limit itself to reinforcing the nobles' reactions but offered advice in matters of general policy. Here again, attitudes were being formed, and again extreme circumstances and powerful motivations were required: once the government lost authority and in its weakness threatened to compromise the work of the Revolution, to which the soldiers were devoted, the army responded to Bonaparte's appeal in the belief that it would lead to the re-establishment of the Republic; once again it turned itself into an instrument for a military regime.

We may wonder how the army could have any broad effect on civilian society, since it was set apart in peacetime by the stationing of troops in forts and in wartime by the distance to the theaters of war. It is a mistake to underestimate the influence exerted by retired soldiers on those around them. We have already pointed out that popular uprisings were often led by former soldiers. This was frequently the case in France in the seventeenth century and in Russia, where Pugachev's revolt in 1771 was partly a military uprising. Usually former soldiers were among the leaders of protests because of the military competence they were assumed to have.

Retired officers and soldiers in France at the end of the eighteenth century retained the honor of their connection with a profession that was becoming increasingly demanding, and they remained in contact with the army by the pensions that were granted more generously and regularly after 1764: full pay for those who had served twenty-four years, half-pay for those with sixteen years of service. And pensioned soldiers were given a new uniform every eight years. Some former soldiers could not re-establish themselves in society and sank into lives of crime, but their number was probably diminishing. Many, on the other hand, found employment with constabulary forces, on public *fermes générales*, in the royal mail service, or as town watchmen, gamekeepers, or gatekeepers. Others became innkeepers or tavern-owners. Most left the army with some familiarity with administrative practices. Their pension enabled them to marry well and set themselves up in some calling, and they were apt to exert considerable influence. The fathers of Beaumarchais and Babeuf had been soldiers, if only for a short time.

Men who had been strongly affected by their army service met often—easily enough, as most of them lived in towns. Particularly if they had certain campaign experiences in common—like those few who had taken part in the American Revolution, for example—former officers and men frequently established firm friendships. There is little doubt that such ex-servicemen played a significant part in the origins and progress of the French Revolution.

Nothing similar took place in other countries, probably because soldiers who might act as praetorians, ex-soldiers who could become propaganda agents, or an army that might assume political power were simply potential factors that could develop real force only in exceptional circumstances.

Conclusion

MEDIEVAL EUROPEAN society was a military society. After 1500, arms retained an element of social prestige, especially because for some time western rulers with fragile monetary economies bound ownership of land to military service. This solution was adopted at the end of the medieval period by the Ottomans and, later, in Sweden with the *Indelningsverket* system and in the military districts of Austria. Military activity, however, involved more people than those in regular army service; it was the symbol of traditional liberties. The nobility was not alone in this feeling, and until the seventeenth century, towns and provinces in the western countries protected the existence of their militias, which were considered to be guarantees of their rights.

In effect, hierarchies of military power were established by sovereigns, feudal nobles, and urban republics, an arrangement that produced whole troops of private soldiers; in the western monarchies these remained at the level of personal retinues of loyal attendants or hired followers, but in central Europe they became the formative elements for national armies. The situation was favorable for the kind of internal civil warfare that was epitomized by the Religious Wars in sixteenth-century France and the Thirty Years War from 1618 to 1648. Military "presence" was widespread and dominant in many countries.

The situation changed gradually with the expanding economic horizons, the growth of the States, and the evolution taking place in military arts. Thus it is not surprising that Italy was the first country to manifest the decline of the profession of arms, in terms of social values. Delayed by religious conflicts in western Europe, expanding government power was by the seventeenth century putting an end to private troops, causing the dispersal of town militias or their incorporation into royal military systems, and dispensing with the services of the *condottieri* or military contractors. These tendencies spread into the countries of central and eastern Europe, although to its misfortune Poland did not follow the modern trends.

After the fifteenth century the greater numbers of troops and the improvement in weapons increased the costs of maintaining armies, making such an effort possible only for rulers with adequate gold or silver resources within their territories or with sufficient tax revenues. Changes in military techniques required greater control over the men in the permanent armies, and the aristocracy grew less interested in serving, supporting the new professionalism only on the condition that they were granted a near-monopoly of officers' positions. At the same time the troops, given more consistent treatment, were housed in barracks and in other ways separated from civilian society: the distinction grew greater between civilians and the military.

Changing attitudes were overturning social values, meanwhile, and wealth and talent became more highly valued than high birth and skill with weapons. In the western countries military careers were less frequently chosen, and civilians were now predominant in governments as well as in society. In central and eastern Europe, on the other hand, only those aristocracies whose land-based power was benefiting from the economic expansion adopted the new attitudes. In serving the States (or sometimes controlling them), noblemen accepted the military character imposed by the rulers on their nations.

While eastern and central European societies tended to become more "military" as they followed the lead of government
systems, in western Europe we find military social groups within
but distinct from society as a whole. It took the national wars set
off by the French Revolution to re-establish tighter, though temporary, links between armies and societies. In the end, the widespread, nearly omnipresent militarization that we see in the
Europe of 1914 came about only with the adoption of the idea of
universal military service by societies that were no longer military
in nature.

WORKS CITED AND
RECOMMENDED BIBLIOGRAPHY

GENERAL

An important source for general information about the history of armies is *The New Cambridge Modern History* series. Certain volumes contain chapters specifically concerned with armies. Particularly recommended are the following:

Vol. 4, *The Decline of Spain and the Thirty Years War* (1970):
  "Military Forces and Warfare," by J. W. Wijns, pp. 202–25.
Vol. 6, *The Rise of Great Britain and Russia*, ed. by J. S. Bromley (1970):
  "Introduction"; "The Art of War on Land," by D. G. Chandler,
  pp. 741–62; "Soldiers and Civilians," by John W. Stoye, pp. 762–90.
Vol. 7, *The Old Regime* (1957): "The Armed Forces and the Art of War,"
  by Eric Robson, pp. 163–90.
Vol. 8, *The American and French Revolutions* (1965): "Armies," by J. R.
  Western, pp. 190–218.

Additional general works used in this study and recommended are:

Boudet, J., ed. *Histoire universelle des armées*. Vols. 2, 3. Paris, 1965.
Bouthoul, G. *Traité de polémologie: Sociologie des guerres*. New ed.
  Paris, 1970.
Dupuy, R. Ernest, and Dupuy, Trevor N. *The Encyclopedia of Military
  History*. New York, 1970.
Livet, G. "La guerre de Trente ans." In *Que Sais-je?* Paris, 1963.
Vagts, Alfred. A *History of Militarism*. 2d ed. New York, 1959.

INDIVIDUAL COUNTRIES

There are many national histories to choose from. Most, however, give more attention to military events and military institutions than to relationships between armies and societies. From this latter point of view, their value varies.

FRANCE

Babeau, Albert A. *La vie militaire sous l'Ancien Régime.* 2 vols. Paris, 1890.

Chagniot, J. "Le problème du maintien de l'ordre à Paris au XVIIIe siècle." *Bulletin de la société d'Histoire moderne*, no. 3 (1974), pp. 33–45.

Contamine, Philippe. *Guerre, etat et société à la fin du Moyen Age: Etudes sur les armées des rois de France, 1337–1494.* Paris, 1972.

Corvisier, André. *L'armée française de la fin du XVIIe siècle au ministère de Choiseul: Le soldat.* 2 vols. Paris, 1964.

——. *Les Français et l'armée sous Louis XIV, d'après les mémoires des intendants, 1697–1698.* Paris, 1975.

——. "Les généraux de Louis XIV et leur origine sociale." *XVIIe siècle*, 1959, pp. 23–53.

——. "Quelques aspects sociaux des milices bourgeoises au XVIIIe siècle." *Annales de la Faculté des Lettres et Sciences humaines de Nice*, 1969, pp. 242–77.

——. "Hiérarchie militaire et hiérarchie sociale à la veille de la Révolution." *Revue internationale d'histoire militaire*, no. 2 (1970), pp. 77–91.

——. "Vocation militaire, misère et niveau d'instruction au XVIIIe siècle: Les limites de la méthode quantitative." In *Actes du XCIIIe Congrès national des Sociétés savantes*, vol. 2, pp. 269–86. Paris, 1971.

——. "La société militaire et l'enfant." *Enfant et société, Annales de démographie historique*, 1973, pp. 327–43.

——. "La mort du soldat depuis la fin du Moyen Age." *Revue historique*, July-Sept. 1975, pp. 3–30.

Eccles, W. J. "The Social, Economic, and Political Significance of the Military Establishment in New France." *Canadian Historical Review*, 1971, no. 1.

Etudes d'histoire militaire, XVIIe–XXe siècles. In *Revue d'histoire moderne et contemporaire*, Jan.-Mar. 1973. (Studies by Blanchard, Chaboche, Chagniot, Devos, Waksman.)

Girard, G. *Racolage et milice, 1701–1715.* Paris, 1921.

Hennet, L. *Les compagnies de cadets-gentilshommes et les écoles militaires.* Paris, 1889.

Léonard, E. G. *L'armée et ses problèmes au XVIIIe siècle.* Paris, 1958.

Serman, S. W., and Bertaud, J.-P. "Vie et psychologie des combattants et gens de guerre, questions de méthodes et de documentation compris l'iconographie, armée française de terre, officiers, sous-officiers et soldats, 1635–1945." In *Mémoires et communications de la Commission française d'histoire militaire*, directed by General F. Gambiez, vol. 1. Paris, 1970.

Tuetey, L. *Les officiers sous l'Ancien Régime*. Paris, 1908.

Yardeni, Myriam. *La conscience national en France pendant les guerres de Religion*, 1559–1598. Paris and Louvain, 1971.

GERMANY AND AUSTRIA

Barker, Thomas. "Military Enterprisership and Absolutismus, Habsburg Models." *Journal of European Studies*, no. 4 (1974), pp. 19–42.

——. "Officer Recruitment in the Habsburg Army of the Seventeenth and Early Eighteenth Centuries." Paper presented at the International Colloquium on Military History at Montpellier, 1974.

Bodart, G. *Militär historisches Kriegslexikon, 1618–1905*. Vienna and Leipzig, 1908.

Büsch, Otto. *Militärsystem und Sozialleben im alten Preussen*. Berlin, 1962.

Demeter, K. *Das deutsche Offizierkorps in Gesellschaft und Staat, 1650–1945*. Frankfurt, 1964.

Duffy, Christopher. "Recruitment and Mentality in the Army of Maria Theresa, 1740–1780." Paper presented at the International Colloquium on Military History at Montpellier, 1974.

Franz, G. *Der dreissigjährige Krieg und das deutsche Volk*. 3d ed. Stuttgart, 1961.

Frauenholz, E. von. *Entwicklungsgeschichte des deutschen Heerwesen*. Vols. 2, 3. Munich, 1936–1939.

Harms, Richard. *Landmiliz und stehendes Heer in Kurmainz, namentlich in 18. Jahrhundert*. Göttingen, 1909.

Heischmann, Eugen. *Die Anfange des stehendes Heeres in Oesterreich*. Vienna, 1925.

Hermann, C. H. *Deutsche Militärgeschichte, eine Einführung*. Frankfurt, 1966.

Jany, C. *Geschichte der königlichen preussischen Armee bis zum Jahre 1807*. 3 vols. Berlin, 1928.

Kessel, E. *Der deutsche Soldat in den stehenden Heeren des Absolutismus*. Berlin and Leipzig, 1937.

Liebe, G. *Der Soldat in der deutschen Vergangenheit*. Leipzig, 1899.

Linnebach, K. *Deutsche Heeresgeschichte*. Hamburg, 1935.

Redlich, F. *The German Military Enterpriser and His Work Force.* 2 vols. Wiesbaden, 1964.

Ritter, Gerhard. *Staatskunst und Kriegshandwert: Das Problem des "Militarismus" in Deutschland.* Vol. 1. Munich, 1954.

———. *The Sword and the Scepter: The Problem of Militarism in Germany.* Translated by Heinz Norden. Vol. 1: *The Prussian Tradition, 1740–1890.* Miami, Fla., 1969.

Staudinger, K. *Geschichte des Kurbayerischen Heeres, 1651–1777.* 3 vols. Munich, 1901, 1905, 1907.

Wrede, A. von. *Geschichte der kaiserliche und königliche Wehrmacht von 1618 bis zum Ende des XIX. Jahrhunderts.* Vols. 1, 3, 4. Vienna, 1898.

GREAT BRITAIN

Boynton, Lindsay. *The Elizabethan Militia, 1558–1638.* London and Toronto, 1967.

Clark, George N. *War and Society in the Seventeenth Century.* Cambridge, 1958.

Cruickshank, C. G. *Elizabeth's Army.* 2d ed. London and Oxford, 1966.

Firth, C. H. *Cromwell's Army.* 2d ed. London, 1912.

Fortescue, John W. *A History of the British Army.* 13 vols. London, 1910–1935.

Goring, J. J. *The Military Obligations of the English People, 1511–1558.* London, 1955.

Scouller, R. E. *The Armies of Queen Anne.* Oxford, 1966.

Stone, Lawrence. *Social Change and Revolution in England, 1540–1640.* London, 1965.

Western, J. R. *The English Militia in the Eighteenth Century.* London and Toronto, 1965.

HUNGARY

d'Eszlary, C. *Histoire des institutions publiques hongroises.* Paris, 1959–1968. Vol. 3, pp. 145–77.

ITALY

Brancaccio, Nicola. *L'Esercito del veccio Piemonte.* Rome, 1922.

Pieri, P. *Guerra e politica negli scrittori italiani.* Milan, 1955.

Quazza, Guido. *Le riforme in Piemonte nella prima meta del settecento.* 2 vols. Modena, 1957.

NETHERLANDS

Henne, A. *Histoire du règne de Charles Quint en Belgique.* Brussels, 1858. Vol. 3, pp. 35–223.

Ruwet, J. *Soldats des régiments nationaux au XVIIIe siècle: Notes et documents.* Brussels, 1962.

Terlinden, C. *Histoire militaire des Belges.* 2d ed. Vol. I. Brussels, 1965.

Van Houtee, Hubert. *Les occupations étrangères en Belgique sous l'Ancien Régime.* 2 vols. Ghent and Paris, 1930.

OTTOMAN EMPIRE

Few studies are available other than general histories.

Sugar, Peter F. "The Ottoman 'Professional Prisoners' on the Western Borders of the Empire in the Sixteenth and Seventeenth Centuries." *Etudes balkaniques*, no. 2 (1971).

War, Technology, and Society in the Middle East. Edited by V. J. Parry and M. E. Yapp. Oxford, 1975.

POLAND

Histoire militaire de la Pologne: Problèmes choisis. Under the direction of the Minister of National Defense. Warsaw, 1970. Note especially the following articles:

Teodorczyk, J. "L'armée polonaise dans la première moitié du XVIIe siècle."

Wimmer, J. "L'infanterie de l'armée polonaise aux XVe–XVIIIe siècles."

Revue international d'histoire militaire comparée, no. 12 (1952). The entire volume is devoted to Poland. Note particularly the following articles:

Kukiel, M. "Origine de la stratégie et de la tactique des insurrections polonaises aux XVIIIe et XIXe siècles."

Sawczynski, A. "Origine des institutions militaires polonaises au XVIIe siècle."

Slaskowski, O. "L'art militaire polonais aux XVIe et XVIIe siècles."

Wimmer, J. "Les procédés de recrutement et la mentalité du soldat polonais au XVIIe siècle." Paper presented at the International Colloquium on Military History at Montpellier, 1974.

RUSSIA

Beskrovnyj, L. G. *Russkaja Armija i Flot v XVIII veke*. Moscow, 1958.
Hellie, Richard. *Enserfment and Military Change in Muscovy*. Chicago, 1971.

SPAIN

Bazy J.-P.-A. *Etat militaire de la monarchie espagnole sous le règne de Philippe IV: Les mercenaires au XVIIe siècle*. Poitiers, 1864.
Clonard, S. de. *Historia organica de las armas de infanteria y caballeria espanolas*. Vols. 3, 4. Madrid, 1851.
Parker, Geoffrey. *The Army of Flanders and the Spanish Road, 1567–1659*. Cambridge, 1972.
Quatrefages, R. "Le Tercio, 1567–1577." Thèse de 3e cycle, Paris-Sorbonne, 1975.

SWEDEN

Ahslund, B. "L'armée de soldats cultivateurs de Charles XI de Suède." *Armi antiche*, 1972, pp. 311–40.
Arteus, H. G. "Some Methodological Problems Confronting Research on the Social Recruitment of Commissioned Officers in Eighteenth-century Sweden." Paper presented at the International Colloquium on Military History at Montpellier, 1974.
Nordmann, C. *Grandeur et liberté de la Suède, 1660–1792*. Paris and Louvain, 1971 (*passim*, especially pp. 87–94).
Roberts, Michael. "The Military Revolution." In *Essays in Swedish History*. London, 1967.

UNITED PROVINCES

Ten Raa, F. G. J., and De Bas, F. *Het staatsche Leger, 1568–1795*. Vol. 8, no. 3. Breda, 1964.

INDEX

Addison, Joseph, 14
Alba [Alva], Fernando Alvarez de Toledo, duke of, 79
Alberoni, Giulio, cardinal, 17
Anne of Austria, queen of France, 192
Arc, Philippe, chevalier d', 103, 167, 189
Argenson, Marc Pierre de Voyer de Paulmy, comte d', 166
argent du roi, 42, 133
armies: numerical strength. *See* military strength
arrière-ban, 8, 26, 28
Assas, Louis, chevalier d', 185
Aulic Council of War, 38, 76, 104
Austria, 19; army, 20, 59, 104–5, 112–13, 115, 121–22, 142, 147–48, 157; war office, 75–76, 122
Austrian Netherlands: army, 28, 50, 114, 121, 141, 147. *See also* Netherlands, the

Bade [Baden], Louis-Guillaume, margrave of, 48
barracks, 80, 82, 124, 125, 189
banderia, 27, 37
Basville, Nicolas Lamoignon de, 32
Bavaria: army, 20, 30, 55, 147, 156, 175, 176
Bayard, chevalier, 98, 185
Belle-Isle, Charles Louis Auguste Fouquet, duc de, 12, 124
Bernardi, and military school, 106
Bernard [Bernhard] of Saxe-Weimar, 44
billeting of troops, 79–80. *See also* barracks
Bohan, baron de, 103
Bohemia, 19, 59
Bonaparte, Napoleon, 125, 193

bonuses, enlistment, 44–45, 69, 133
Bouillon, Henri de la Tour d'Auvergne, duc de, 106
Bourbon, Charles, duc de, 5
Brantôme, Pierre de Bourdeilles, seigneur de, 161, 183, 184
Broussel, Pierre, 192
Burlamachi, banker, 43

cadet companies, 103, 106–7, 108, 165
Castiglione, Balthazar, 4
Cervantes Saavedra, Miguel de, 11
Chamlay, marquis de, 77
champ de mai, 25–26
Charles I, king of England, 35, 192
Charles II, king of England, 14, 76
Charles III, king of Spain, 155
Charles IV, duke of Lorraine, 44
Charles V, Holy Roman emperor, 23–24, 66
Charles VII, king of France, 29, 49, 73–74
Charles XI, king of Sweden, 11, 53
Charles XII, king of Sweden, 53, 88
children of soldiers, 144, 175
China: armies, 1
chivalry, 11, 98, 183
Choiseul, Etienne François, duc de, 12, 103
Christina, queen of Sweden, 84
Cisneros, Francisco Jiménez de, cardinal, 29
civilians, rights of, 78, 186
civilians and troops, 81–82
coast guard, 33
Colbert, Jean Baptiste, 86, 164
Coligny, Gaspard de Chatillon, comte, 192
commissaries, 74, 151
concordat, 101–2, 158

205